A Bible Study by

Melissa Spoelstra

First Corinthians

Living Love
When We Disagree

Leader Guide

Abingdon Women / Nashville

FIRST CORINTHIANS
Living Love When We Disagree, Leader Guide

ISBN 978-1-5018-0170-9

16 17 18 19 20 21 22 23 24 25—10 9 8 7 6 5 4 3 2 1
MANUFACTURED IN THE UNITED STATES OF AMERICA

Contents

About the Author 4

Introduction 5

Getting Started 9

Tips for Tackling Five Common Challenges 12

Basic Leader Helps 17

Introductory Session 18

Week 1: In Christ Alone (1 Corinthians 1–2) 20

    Digging Deeper Week 1 Highlights: My Town 25

Week 2: Growing Up (1 Corinthians 3–5) 27

    Digging Deeper Week 2 Highlights: Unstuck 32

Week 3: Everybody's Doing It (1 Corinthians 6–8) 34

    Digging Deeper Week 3 Highlights: Defining Church 39

Week 4: Beyond Ourselves (1 Corinthians 9–11) 41

    Digging Deeper Week 4 Highlights: Loving Boundaries 46

Week 5: Living Love (1 Corinthians 12–14) 48

    Digging Deeper Week 5 Highlights: A Controversial Gift 53

    Digging Deeper Week 5 Highlights: The Sound of Silence 55

Week 6: Real Life (1 Corinthians 15–16) 57

    Digging Deeper Week 6 Highlights: Afterlife 62

Video Viewer Guide Answers 64

About the Author

Melissa Spoelstra is a popular women's conference speaker, Bible teacher, and writer who is madly in love with Jesus and passionate about studying God's Word and helping women of all ages seek Christ and know Him more intimately through serious Bible study. Having a degree in Bible theology, she enjoys teaching God's Word to the body of Christ and traveling to diverse groups and churches across the nation, even to Nairobi, Kenya, for a women's prayer conference. Melissa is the author of *Joseph: The Journey to Forgiveness*, *Jeremiah: Daring to Hope in an Unstable World*, and *Total Family Makeover: 8 Steps to Making Disciples at Home*. She has published articles in *ParentLife, Women's Spectrum*, and *Just Between Us*, and writes a regular blog in which she shares her musings about what God is teaching her on any given day. She lives in Dublin, Ohio, with her pastor husband, Sean, and their four kids: Zach, Abby, Sara, and Rachel.

Follow Melissa:

Twitter	@MelSpoelstra
Instagram	@Daring2Hope
Facebook	@AuthorMelissaSpoelstra
Her blog	MelissaSpoelstra.com (check here also for event dates and booking information)

Introduction

Living love isn't easy, especially when we disagree. We can find ourselves disagreeing or debating with family, friends, coworkers, and even strangers on social media about everything from food choices and parenting styles to politics and religion. Often we find ourselves divided—even as Christians. How can we work out our differences with humility and grace, always showing the love of Christ, while still remaining true to what we believe?

The Apostle Paul wrote a letter to the church in Corinth about this very thing, because they struggled with their own set of issues and had a reputation for conflict. Paul urged the church in Corinth to "be of one mind, united in thought and purpose" (1 Corinthians 1:10). He essentially called them to live love—even when they disagreed. Chapter 13, known as the love chapter, wasn't included to be a nice poem for weddings. Instead, it was written to urge Christians living in a pagan and diverse culture to approach one another with the love of Christ. It calls us to do the same.

Regrettably, we often exercise the opposite of that kind of love, choosing instead to keep a record of wrongs or to make rude comments—whether in person or on social media. The truth is, we can never demonstrate this supernatural love and kindness with those who disagree with us apart from Jesus. Paul acknowledged this truth, mentioning the name of Jesus nine times in the first nine verses of this letter alone! He knew that we desperately need Christ at the center of our personal lives, including our interactions with others. Our unity comes only through Christ and His love. That is the focus of this study.

As we dive deep into Paul's letter, we will explore how we can

- Deal with our differences in a loving way without compromising our convictions
- Achieve harmony while maintaining our diversity
- Consider the ways that the surrounding culture impacts our beliefs
- Agree to disagree on matters of preference and opinion
- Humbly listen to others with views different than our own
- Embrace ambiguity in some areas, acknowledging that our view is often partial and incomplete
- Demonstrate to all that love is the greatest thing, which never fails

Using This Leader Guide

This leader guide is provided to help you lead your group on this journey to learn how to live love even when we disagree. Whether you choose to follow this guide step by step, modify its contents to meet your group's needs and preferences, or simply peruse it to find a few helpful tips, questions, and ideas, you will find in these pages some valuable tools for creating a successful group experience. Here is a quick overview of what is included:

Getting Started: This is a list of strategies, options, and introductory information that will help you ensure good organization and communication. You will want to review this material and communicate relevant information to group members prior to your group session for Week 1, either via e-mail or in an introductory session (see more about this in Getting Started). Or you might consider adding fifteen to thirty minutes to your first session for reviewing some of these important housekeeping details. Whichever option you choose, be sure that group members have the opportunity to purchase books and complete Week 1 before your session for Week 1.

Tips for Tackling Five Common Challenges: This section includes ideas for addressing recurring issues that come up when leading a group. Every leader knows that some group dynamics can be difficult to tackle. What will you do when one person dominates the discussion or cuts off another person who is speaking? All eyes will be on you to see how you will intervene in or ignore these situations. Be sure to check out these five common challenges and ideas to help when you encounter them.

Basic Leader Helps: This list of basic leader tips will help you prepare for and lead each group session.

Session Outlines: Six adaptable outlines are provided to help guide your group time each week. Each begins with a "Leader Prep" section to assist with preparation.

Digging Deeper Article Highlights: These are highlights from the full-length Digging Deeper articles found online at AbingdonPress.com/FirstCorinthians, in which you will find second-level, concise information your group members do not have in their participant books, such as cultural insights, background information, commentary, and so forth. (Be sure to read the full articles online prior to your group session.) As you dialogue with God about leading each session, ask Him what parts of the corresponding Digging Deeper article He might want you to share with the group. This will give participants an opportunity to continue to learn new insights in your time together each week. Feel free to point your group members to the online articles in class or via e-mail, Facebook, Twitter, or other social media.

This study is designed for six weeks, with an optional introductory session. Or, if desired, you may choose to extend the study to eight or twelve weeks; see the options included in Getting Started. Again, whichever option you choose, be sure that group members have the opportunity to purchase participant books and complete Week 1 before your session for Week 1.

Each of the session outlines in this book may be used for a 60-minute, 90-minute, or 120-minute session. The following formats are offered as templates that you may modify for your group:

60-Minute Format
Welcome/Fellowship (2 minutes)
All Play (3 minutes)
Digging Deeper Insights (4 minutes)
Prayer (1 minute)
Video (25 minutes)
Group Discussion (20 minutes)
Prayer Requests (5 minutes)

90-Minute Format
Welcome/Fellowship (5-10 minutes)
All Play (5 minutes)
Digging Deeper Insights (4 minutes)
Prayer (1 minute)
Video (25 minutes)
Group Discussion (25 minutes)
Optional Group Activity (5-10 minutes)
Prayer Requests (10 minutes)

120-Minute Format
Welcome/Fellowship (15-20 minutes)
All Play (5-10 minutes)
Digging Deeper Insights (4 minutes)
Prayer (1 minute)
Video (25 minutes)
Group Discussion (30 minutes)
Optional Group Activity (5-10 minutes)
Prayer Requests (15-20 minutes)

As you can see, the basic elements remain the same in each format: a welcome/fellowship time, an "All Play" icebreaker question that everyone can answer, an opportunity to share insights with the group from the week's Digging Deeper article, a video segment, group discussion, and prayer time. The 90-minute and 120-minute options offer longer times for fellowship, discussion, and prayer plus an Optional Group Activity. If you choose not to do the group activity, you may add that time to another element of the session, such as group discussion or prayer. (See Getting Started for notes about including food, planning for childcare, and other important organizational details.)

If you are new to leading Bible studies and/or would like to have a framework to follow, the session outlines will guide you. Note that more discussion questions have been provided than you may have time to include. Before the session, choose the questions you want to cover and put a check mark beside them. Page references are provided for those questions that relate to specific questions or activities in the participant book. For these questions, invite group members to turn in their participant books to the pages indicated.

If you are a seasoned group leader looking only for a few good questions or ideas, I encourage you to take what you want and leave the rest. After all, you know your group better than I do! Ask God to show you what areas to focus on from the week's homework and use my discussion outline as a template that you can revise.

Of course, the Holy Spirit knows the content of this study (His Word) and the women in your group better than anyone, so above all I encourage you to lead this study under the Holy Spirit's direction, allowing yourself the freedom to make any changes or adaptations that are helpful or desirable.

I'm so excited that God has called you to lead a group of ladies through Paul's first letter to the church in Corinth. Know that I am praying for you and believing God for the work He will do through your leadership. Now, let's get started!

Melissa

Getting Started

Before your study begins, be sure to review the following introductory information that will help you ensure good organization and communication. You are encouraged to communicate relevant information such as the dates, times, and location for group meetings; when/where/how to purchase books; details regarding childcare and food; expectations and ground rules; and an overview of the study to group members during an introductory session or via e-mail before your session for Week 1.

1. Determine the length of your study. The basic study is designed for six weeks (plus an optional introductory session), but you also can plan for an eight- or twelve-week study.
   - For a six-week study plus an introductory session, use the session guides in this book and the video segments on the DVD. Be sure to distribute books during the introductory session or prior to your session for Week 1.
   - For an eight-week study, add both an introductory session and a closing celebration. In the introductory session, watch the introduction video and spend time getting to know one another, presenting basic housekeeping information, and praying together (use the guide on pages 18-19). For a closing celebration, discuss what you have learned together in a special gathering that includes refreshments or perhaps a brunch, luncheon, or supper. A closing celebration provides an excellent opportunity for ongoing groups to invite friends and reach out to others who might be interested in joining the group for a future study.
   - To allow more time for completing homework, extend the study to twelve weeks. This is especially helpful for groups with mothers of young children or women carrying a heavy work or ministry schedule. With this option, women have two weeks in which to complete each week of homework in the participant book. In your group sessions, watch and discuss the video the first week; then review and discuss homework the next week. Some women find they are better able to complete assignments and digest what they are learning this way.

2. Determine the length of each group session (60, 90, or 120 minutes). See the format templates outlined on page 7.

3. Decide ahead of time if you/your church will purchase participant books that group members can buy in advance during an introductory session or in advance of your first session, or if group members will buy their own books individually. If you expect each member to buy her own book, e-mail group members purchasing information (be sure to note the cost, including tax and shipping if applicable). Consider including online links as well. Be sure to allow enough time for participants to purchase books and complete the readings for Week 1 prior to your session for Week 1.

4. Create a group roster that includes each group member's name, e-mail, mailing address, and primary phone number. (Collect this information through registration, e-mail, or an introductory session.) Distribute copies of the roster to group members prior to or during your first session. A group roster enables group members to stay connected and contact one another freely as needed, such as when taking a meal or sending a card or note to someone who is sick, who has missed several group sessions, or who has had a baby or another significant life event. Group members may want to meet for coffee or lunch to follow up on things shared in the study as well. As women cry and laugh and share life together in a Bible study, their lives will be intertwined, even if for a short time.

5. Make decisions about childcare and food and communicate this information to group members in advance. Will childcare be offered, and will there be a cost associated with it? Will refreshments be served at your gatherings? (*Note*: If your group is meeting for sixty minutes, you will not have time for a formal fellowship time with refreshments. You might consider having refreshments set up early and inviting women to come a few minutes before the session officially begins.) If you choose to have food, the introductory meeting is a good time to pass around a sign-up sheet. In the Bible study group I lead, we like to eat, so we have three women sign up to bring food for each meeting. One brings fruit, another brings bread or muffins, and another brings an egg dish. Your group may want to keep it simple; just be mindful of food allergies and provide choices that will not exclude women.

6. Let group members know what to expect. Those who have never participated in a women's Bible study group may be intimidated, scared, or unsure of what to expect. Friends have told me that when they first came to Bible study, they were concerned they would be called on to pray out loud or expected to know everything in the Bible. Ease group members' concerns up front. Reassure the women that they will not be put on the spot and that they may choose to share as they are comfortable. Encourage participation while fostering a "safe" environment. Laying a few basic ground rules such as these can help you achieve this kind of environment:

    - *Confidentiality.* Communicate that anything shared in the group is not to be repeated outside of those present in the study. Women need to feel safe to be vulnerable and authentic. When areas of disagreement arise, women will need reassurance that it is okay to hold different positions and they can share without fear that their words will be repeated and evaluated by others outside of the group.

    - *Sensitivity.* Talk about courtesy, which includes practices such as refraining from interrupting, monopolizing, or trying to "fix" shared problems. Women want to be heard, not told what to do, when they share an issue in their lives. If they have advice to share with an individual, ask them to speak with the person privately after study. When studying God's Word, some differences of opinion are bound to arise as to interpretation and/or application. This is a good place to sharpen one another and respectfully disagree so that you may grow and understand different viewpoints. Remind the women that it's okay to question and see things differently; however, they must be kind and sensitive to the feelings of others.

- *Purpose.* The primary reason you are taking time out of your busy schedules to meet together is to study the Bible. Though your group will pray for, serve, and support one another, your primary focus is to study the Bible. You learn in community from one another as you draw near to God through His Word. Though you may want to plan a service or social activity during the course of your study, these times should be secondary to your study time together. If group members express a desire for the group to do more outreach, service, or socials, gently remind them of the primary reason you gather.

7. Before the study begins, provide a short preview of the study's content, summarizing highlights in an e-mail or introductory session. Whet the appetite for what is to come by sharing (or reading) parts of the introduction from the participant book. Although Paul wrote his letter to a specific group of people in a specific culture, the struggle to get along is just as relevant today. Consider sharing a personal story that relates to the study's theme. What has been happening in your life recently that has given you an opportunity to live love when you disagree? As you are enthusiastic about getting into God's Word together, your members will catch your contagious desire to focus on our unity in Christ even in the midst of conflict.

8. If you are having an introductory session, show the introduction video and open the floor for women to share in response to the questions on page 19.

9. Read the Week 1 Digging Deeper Article "My Town" at AbingdonPress.com /FirstCorinthians (highlights on pages 25-26), which explores how the culture shaped the original audience of Paul's letter. Share these insights in an introductory session or during the Digging Deeper Insights segment of your first session.

10. Be sure to communicate to participants that they are to read Week 1 in the participant book prior to your session for Week 1. Review the options for study found in the introduction to the participant book and encourage participants to choose the options they plan to complete and then share this information with someone in the group for accountability.

Tips for Tackling
Five Common Challenges

Challenge #1: Preparation

Do you know that feeling when Bible study is in two days and you haven't even finished the homework, much less prepared for the group session? We've all been there. I'm hurried, scattered, and less confident when I haven't dedicated the proper time for preparation. I check myself with a little acronym when I prepare to lead: S-S-S. Many years ago I was asked to lead a segment on teacher training for a group of VBS leaders. I remember asking the Lord, "What are the most important things to remember when we handle your Word to teach?" As I sat listening, He gave me this process of S-S-S that has stuck with me through the years. It looks like this:

S – Savior. Know your Savior. We must spend time talking, listening, and staying closely connected with Jesus in order to lead well. As we keep our walk with Him close and vibrant, we can then hear His voice about how to structure our lesson, what questions to ask, and which verses in His Word to focus on.

S – Story. Know your story. Though God has been gracious to me when I have winged it, I feel the most freedom with God's truth when I have prepared thoroughly. Try not to cram in multiple days of homework at one time. Let it sink into your soul by reading curiously and slowly. Go back to areas that especially strike you and allow God to use His Word in your heart and mind so that you can teach with authenticity.

S – Students. Know your students. Who are these women God has given you to shepherd? Are they struggling with finances, relationships, or body image issues? Are they mature Christ-followers who need to be challenged to go deeper in their study of God's Word or seekers who need extra explanations about where the books of the Bible are located? Most likely, you will be teaching to a wide range of backgrounds as well as emotional and spiritual maturity levels, and you will need God's wisdom and guidance to inspire them.

Challenge #2: Group Dynamics

Have you experienced that uncomfortable feeling when you ask a discussion question and a long silence settles over the group? With your eyes begging someone to break the ice, you wonder if you should let the question linger or jump in with your own answer. Other problems with group dynamics surface when Silent Suzy never contributes to the conversation because Talking Tammy answers every question. What does a good leader do in these situations? While every group has a unique vibe, I have found these general concepts very helpful in facilitating discussion:

First of all, a good leader asks questions. Jesus was our greatest example. He definitely taught spiritual truths, but one of His most effective methods was asking questions. As leaders, we must be intentional askers and listeners. I try to gauge myself throughout the discussion by reflecting often on this simple question: "Am I doing all the talking?" When I find I am hearing my own voice too much, I make a point to ask and listen more. Even if waiting means a little silence hangs in the air, eventually someone will pipe up and share. Women learn from each other's insights and experiences; we rob them of others' comments when we monopolize as leaders.

Now what about Talking Tammy? She not only answers every question but also makes a comment after each woman shares something (often relating to one of her own experiences). Try one of these transitional statements:

- "Thanks Tammy, let's see if someone else has some insight as well."
- "Let's hear from someone who hasn't shared yet today."
- "Is there anyone who hasn't talked much today who would be willing to answer this question?"

The hope is that Talking Tammy will realize that she has had a lot of floor time.

Sometimes Talking Tammy also struggles to "land the plane." She can't find a stopping place in her story. Help her out by jumping in when she takes a breath and make a summary statement for her. For example, "I hear you saying that you could relate to the Corinthian believers in their disagreements. It's difficult to be loving when we see things so differently. Anyone else find the problems in the church at Corinth resonating in a similar way?" Occasionally I have had to take someone aside in a loving way and address her amount of talking. Pray hard and be gentle, but address the issue.

I once had several ladies leave the group because they were so frustrated by the continual barrage of talking by one woman in particular. Some of her many comments were insensitive and offensive to others in the room. I don't like confrontation, so I didn't want to address it. However, God grew me as a leader to speak loving truth even when it hurts for the benefit of those we are called to shepherd.

Sometimes even more challenging than Talking Tammy is Silent Suzy. We must walk a fine line as leaders, not putting on the spot those women who are uncomfortable talking in front of others. I have scared women away by being too direct. So how do we get Silent Suzy to talk without singling her out? Here are some ideas:

- If she is new to the study, don't push her during the first few sessions. Let her feel safe and get comfortable. Never call on her to pray out loud or single her out with a pointed question. I once said, "I want to know what Suzy thinks about this." All eyes turned on her, and I'll never forget the tears welling in the corners of her eyes as she said she wasn't comfortable being called on. She didn't come back to the group after that incident. I learned a valuable lesson from that Silent Suzy—don't push!
- Listen with recall as she answers the All Play question that everyone is asked to answer. Watch for an opportunity to talk about something she has shared with a follow-up question that doesn't pry.

- Take her out for coffee and get to know her. With time, she might warm up and begin to contribute to the discussion. Through a deepened relationship, you'll get a better read on whether you should encourage her to talk.

Challenge #3: Prayer Requests

How often do we run out of time when sharing prayer requests, leaving us no time to actually pray? How do you handle those women who aren't comfortable praying out loud? What if your group has fifteen to thirty women, and just listening to everyone's prayer request takes half an hour? It's so important to take the time to hear what is going on in each other's lives and to pray for one another. Here are some creative ideas I have learned from others to help keep prayer time fresh:

- As women enter the room, direct them to take an index card or sticky note and write their prayer request on it. Then during prayer time, each woman can read her request aloud, and pass it to the woman on the right for her to keep in her Bible as a reminder to pray for the request until they meet again.
- Ask someone to record all the prayer requests and e-mail them to the group each week.
- If you have a small group, use a one- or two-minute sand timer when you are short on time. (Look in your game closet for one of these.) Lightheartedly tell each woman that she has one or two minutes to share her request so that each woman can have a turn. (You might want to flip it over again if tears accompany the request.)
- If you have more than ten women, divide into two or three groups for prayer time. Assign a leader who will facilitate, keep the group on track, and follow up. Sometimes our prayer group has gone out for breakfast together or gathered in someone's home to watch the teaching video again.
- Have women pick one or two partners and split into small groups of two or three to share prayer requests and pray for each other.
- Have an open time of popcorn prayer. This means let women spontaneously pray one-sentence prayers as they feel led.
- After everyone shares requests, ask each woman to pray for the woman on her right. Clearly say that if anyone is uncomfortable praying out loud, she can pray silently and then squeeze the hand of the woman next to her.
- Another option is to close the group in prayer yourself or ask a few women you know are comfortable praying in front of others to pray for the requests mentioned. Always be sensitive to others and affirm that they will not be looked down on if they don't like to pray out loud.

Making a change in your prayer time occasionally keeps it from becoming routine or boring. Talking with Jesus should be fresh and real. Taking an intentional, thoughtful approach to this important time of your study will add great value to your time together.

Challenge #4: Developing Leaders

Women's Bible study groups are a great avenue for fulfilling the 2-2-2 principle, which comes from 2 Timothy 2:2: "You have heard me teach things that have been confirmed by many reliable witnesses. Now teach these truths to other trustworthy people who will be able to pass them on to others." As a leader, God calls us to help raise up other leaders.

Is there a woman in your group who is capable of leading? How can you come alongside her and help equip her to be an even better leader? Wonderful women have invested in me through the 2-2-2 principle, even before I knew that term. As an apprentice, I watched them lead. They gave me opportunities to try leading without handing the full reins over to me. Then they coached and corrected me. I have since had the privilege of mentoring several apprentices in my Bible study group and watching them go on to lead their own groups. This is multiplying leaders and groups, and God loves it!

Here is the 2-2-2 principle as laid out by Dave and Jon Ferguson in their book *Exponential*.[1] (My notes are added within brackets.)

- I DO. You WATCH. We TALK.
- I DO. You HELP. We TALK. [Have your apprentice lead a prayer group or an activity or portion of the session.]
- You DO. I HELP. We TALK. [Ask your apprentice to lead one session with you assisting with facilitation alongside her.]
- You DO. I WATCH. We TALK. [Give your apprentice full ownership for leading a session and resist the urge to jump in and take over.]
- You DO. Someone else WATCHES. [As God leads over time, encourage your apprentice to start her own Bible study group.]

My mentor and I led a Bible study group together for years. As the group grew larger, we both sensed God leading us to multiply the group, forming two groups. It was painful as we missed studying and working with each other. However, God blessed and used both groups to reach more women. Then a woman in my group felt called to lead her own study. She worried that no one would come to her group. She asked many questions as we worked through the 2-2-2 principle. Her first group meeting included eighteen women who now, five years later, still love meeting together. I've seen pictures of them on Facebook enjoying special times together, and I praise God for all that He is doing.

From our one study there are now over five groups of women that meet regularly to study God's Word. This kind of growth begins with commitment to share leadership, follow the 2-2-2 principle, and multiply so that more women can grow in their walk with Christ. Don't miss the opportunity to develop new leaders with intentionality as you model and encourage other women to use their gifts.

Challenge #5: Reaching Out

How do you welcome new women into the group? This is especially tough if yours is an ongoing group that has had the same women in it for years. Newcomers can feel like outsiders if it seems like everyone already knows the unspoken rules of the group. Also, what about those who are finding their way back to God? Are they welcome in the group? While the purpose of the group is primarily Bible study, I've seen the Great Commission of making disciples happen many times through women's groups that meet for Bible study. God's Word will do the transforming work in their lives through the Holy Spirit. We are called to reach out by investing and inviting. Here are some ways a leader can help create an open group:

- End each Bible study with a closing celebration brunch, encouraging the women to bring food and friends. Some ideas for this time together include:
  1. Have an open time when women can share how God worked in their lives through the Bible study.
  2. Have one woman in the group share her testimony of how she came to understand the gospel and how it has been transforming her life recently.
  3. Bring in a speaker from outside the group to share a testimony.
  4. Make it fun! We play a fun group game (such as Fishbowl, Pictionary, or Loaded Questions) and have a white elephant jewelry exchange at Christmas. Women who might think Bible study is a foreign concept can see that you are just a bunch of regular women in pursuit of a supernatural God.
- Leave an empty chair in the group and pray for God to show you someone who needs a group of women she can study the Bible alongside.
- Though the main purpose of the group is Bible study, consider doing a service project together that you can invite other women to participate in (schedules permitting). Our group has made personal care bags for the homeless and also adopted a family at Christmas, which included going shopping for the gifts and wrapping them together. Depending on where God is leading your group, serving together can help put hands and feet to the truths you are learning.
- Socials outside of Bible study also provide an opportunity to invite friends as a non-threatening transition. While the focus of your group is much more than social, planning an occasional social event can be a good way to forge deeper connections. Our Bible study group has gone bowling together, had a backyard barbecue, and planned a girls' night out at a local restaurant. These times together not only help women get to know one another better but also give them a great chance to invite friends. These same friends who attend a social might later try a Bible study session once they have made connections with some of the women in the group.

---

[1] Dave Ferguson and Jon Ferguson, *Exponential: How You and Your Friends Can Start a Missional Church Movement* (Grand Rapids, MI: Zondervan, 2010), 58, 63.

Basic Leader Helps

Preparing for the Sessions

- Check out your meeting space before each group session. Make sure the room is ready. Do you have enough chairs? Do you have the equipment and supplies you need? (See the list of materials needed in each session outline.)
- Pray for your group and each group member by name. Ask God to work in the life of every woman in your group.
- Read and complete the week's readings in the participant book, review the session outline in the leader guide, and read the Digging Deeper article for the week. Put a check mark beside the discussion questions you want to cover and make any notes in the margins that you want to share in your discussion time.

Leading the Sessions

- Personally greet each woman as she arrives. If desired, take attendance using your group roster. (This will assist you in identifying members who have missed several sessions so that you may contact them and let them know they were missed.)
- At the start of each session, ask the women to turn off or silence their cell phones.
- Begin and end on time. Honor the efforts of those who are on time.
- Encourage everyone to participate fully, but don't put anyone on the spot. Invite the women to share as they are comfortable. Be prepared to offer a personal example or answer if no one else responds at first.
- Facilitate but don't dominate. Remember that if you talk most of the time, group members may tend to listen passively rather than to engage personally.
- Try not to interrupt, judge, or minimize anyone's comments or input.
- Remember that you are not expected to be the expert or have all the answers. Acknowledge that all of you are on this journey together, with the Holy Spirit as your leader and guide.
- Encourage good discussion, but don't be timid about calling time on a particular question and moving ahead. Try to end on time. If you are running over, give members the opportunity to leave if they need to. Then wrap up as quickly as you can.
- Be prepared for some women to want to hang out and talk at the end. If you need everyone to leave by a certain time, communicate this at the beginning of the session. If you are meeting in a church during regularly scheduled activities or have arranged for childcare, be sensitive to the agreed-upon ending time.
- Thank the women for coming, and let them know you're looking forward to seeing them next time.

Introductory Session

Note: The regular session outline has been modified for this optional introductory session, which is 60 minutes long.

Leader Prep

Digging Deeper

Read Digging Deeper Week 1, "My Town." Note any interesting facts or insights that you would like to share with the group. (See pages 25-26 for highlights; read the full article online at AbingdonPress.com/FirstCorinthians.)

Materials Needed

- *First Corinthians* DVD and DVD player
- Stick-on nametags and markers (optional)
- Index cards (optional—Prayer Requests)
- Participant books to purchase or distribute

Session Outline

Note: Refer to the format templates on page 7 for suggested time allotments.

Welcome

Offer a word of welcome to the group. If time allows and you choose to provide food, invite the women to enjoy refreshments and fellowship. (Groups meeting for sixty minutes may want to have a time for food and fellowship before the official start time.) Be sure to watch the clock and move to the All Play icebreaker at the appropriate time.

All Play

Ask each group member to complete this sentence: "I love _____." (It doesn't have to be deep; it might be pizza or a new shirt!)

Distribute the participant books, and then have the group turn to the introduction (pages 5-7). Ask volunteers to read one paragraph each until you've read through the entire introduction. Point out the different options for study (page 7) and encourage each woman to prayerfully decide what level of study she would like to complete. Ask: *Based on this introduction, what are you looking forward to about studying First Corinthians?*

Digging Deeper Insights

Share with the group the insights you gained from Digging Deeper Week 1, "My Town" (highlights on pages 25-26; full article at AbingdonPress.com/FirstCorinthians). Share ways that the geography, history, religion, and customs of Corinth influenced the original audience of Paul's letter. Then ask this question: *How has your town shaped you?* If you choose, encourage group members to read the article online.

One option for developing leaders in your group is to invite up to seven women to sign up to read one (or more) of the weekly Digging Deeper articles online, and then have each woman share the highlights of what she learned during the appropriate group session. Create a sign-up sheet that lists each week with the article name and the date of your group session. The pilot group I led did this, and six different women signed up. Some of the women even made handouts that summarized what stood out to them. Others told how that particular week's articles resonated personally with them. This will help you identify potential leaders as well as help pique the women's interest in "digging deeper."

Video

Offer a brief prayer and then play the Introduction video.

Discuss:

- What is something new you learned about Paul or First Corinthians?
- What is one thing you are looking forward to in this study?
- How is the topic of living love when we disagree relevant to your life right now?

Prayer Requests

End by inviting group members to share prayer requests and pray for one another. Use index cards, popcorn prayer, or another prayer technique included in Tips for Tackling Five Common Challenges (pages 12-16) to lead this time with intentionality and sensitivity.

Week 1

IN CHRIST ALONE

1 Corinthians 1–2

Leader Prep

Memory Verse

I appeal to you, dear brothers and sisters, by the authority of our Lord Jesus Christ, to live in harmony with each other. Let there be no divisions in the church. Rather, be of one mind, united in thought and purpose. (1 Corinthians 1:10)

Digging Deeper

If you did not have an introductory session, read Digging Deeper Week 1, "My Town," and note any interesting facts or insights that you would like to share with the group. (See pages 25-26 for highlights; read the full article online at AbingdonPress.com /FirstCorinthians.)

Materials Needed

- *First Corinthians* DVD and DVD player
- Stick-on nametags and markers (optional)
- Paper and pens or pencils (Optional Group Activity)
- Index cards or sticky notes (optional—Scriptures and Prayer Requests)

Session Outline

Note: Refer to the format templates on page 7 for suggested time allotments.

Welcome

Offer a word of welcome to the group. If time allows and you choose to provide food, invite the women to enjoy refreshments and fellowship. (Groups meeting for sixty minutes may want to have a time for food and fellowship before the official start time.) Be sure to watch the clock and move to the All Play icebreaker at the appropriate time.

All Play

Ask each group member to respond briefly to this question: *Who is a person you admire and why?* (It can be a person from history, a contemporary personality, or someone you know personally. Don't think too deeply. This is not the person you admire most but just someone you admire.)

Read aloud or paraphrase:

> *We all have those we look up to as great leaders, moms, teachers, or faithful followers of Jesus. The believers in Corinth also looked up to the apostles and other strong leaders. While people can model great attributes, we must be careful never to elevate the messenger above the message when it comes to the gospel of Christ. Our greatest mentors are those who point us to Jesus rather than themselves. Paul wanted the church at Corinth to depend on Christ alone for their salvation as well as for the power to live out their daily walk of faith. He encouraged them to remember that God's wisdom and the world's wisdom look very different at times.*

Digging Deeper Insights

If you did not have an introductory session, share the insights you gained from Digging Deeper Week 1, "My Town," (highlights on pages 25-26; full article at AbingdonPress .com/FirstCorinthians). Share ways that the geography, history, religion, and customs of Corinth influenced the original audience of Paul's letter. Then ask this question: *How has your town shaped you?* If you choose, encourage group members to read the full article online.

Prayer

Before playing the video segment, ask God to prepare the group to receive His Word and hear IIis voice.

Video

Play the video for Week 1. Invite participants to complete the Video Viewer Guide for Week 1 in the participant book as they watch (pages 42-43). (Answers are provided on page 64 of this book.)

Group Discussion

Video Discussion Questions

- What is the difference between unity and uniformity, and why is this important for us as followers of Christ?
- What does seeing others as holy have to do with living love when we disagree?
- How can the new H_2O—(hope of) heaven, Holy Spirit, optimism—help us navigate our differences and disagreements?

Participant Book Discussion Questions

Note: Page references are provided for those questions that relate to specific questions or activities in the participant book.

Before you begin, invite volunteers to look up the following Scriptures and be prepared to read them aloud when called upon. You might want to write each of the Scripture references on a separate index card or sticky note that you can hand out.

Scriptures: 1 Corinthians 1:1-3; 1 Corinthians 1:10-13; John 17:20-23;
1 Corinthians 1:18-25; Isaiah 29:13-14; 1 Corinthians 1:19; 1 Corinthians 1:31;
Jeremiah 9:23-24; 1 Corinthians 2:1-9; Acts 18:1-11; Isaiah 64:1-4;
1 Corinthians 2:9; 1 Corinthians 2:10-16; John 14:16-17; Philippians 2:5-8;
1 Corinthians 2:16

Day 1: Spiritual Identity

- What are some topics on which Christians today often disagree?
- On page 10 we read, "The question isn't whether we will have disagreements in the church but how we will handle these conflicts." What are some words that describe healthy postures we can take in the midst of disagreement?
- What modern cities come to mind when you read about Corinth? What parallels do you find between Corinthian culture and our culture? (page 11)
- Read 1 Corinthians 1:1-3. Consider the disagreements you have observed within the body of Christ. How could seeing ourselves and one another as holy help with conflict resolution? (Answers will vary; there is no one right answer.) (page 13)

Day 2: Dealing with Divisions

- How do you think social media has impacted our forms of communication in both positive and negative ways?

- Read 1 Corinthians 1:10-13 and refer to the illustration on page 18. Which tendency do you identify with more: skeptic or sheeple? (page 18)
- What are some ways we can take a more balanced approach toward leaders in order to avoid relational idolatry?
- Read John 17:20-23. How have you seen unity expressed among believers in the midst of differing opinions? (page 20)

Day 3: The Foolish Plan of God

- Read 1 Corinthians 1:18-25. Verse 24 says that Christ is the "power of God and the wisdom of God." How do those attributes of Christ encourage you related to any situations you may be dealing with right now?
- Ask if any of the women would be willing to share how they answered this question: "When did you make a personal decision to follow Christ? Or if you've loved Jesus since you were a very young child, when did you begin to understand the message of the cross?" (page 24)
- Read Isaiah 29:13-14 and 1 Corinthians 1:19. From the perspective of hindsight, when and how have God's plans worked out better than your own plans? (page 25)
- When has God's wisdom not been in alignment with what made sense or felt right to you? (page 25)
- Read 1 Corinthians 1:31 and Jeremiah 9:23-24. According to these verses, what are we to boast about? Why is God the only One worth boasting about? (You might read this excerpt from page 28 aloud: "God doesn't want us to live with a distorted view of reality. He is the only One worth boasting about. He isn't a megalomaniac who is obsessed with people boasting about Him; He just favors the truth.")
- What are some character qualities of God you can boast about today?

Day 4: Beyond Imagination

- Read 1 Corinthians 2:1-9. How do you think persuasive words or a demonstrative presentation actually could have been detrimental to the clarity of Paul's message? (Think about times when someone's eloquence was a distraction to you.) (page 30)
- Do you think Paul is saying that we should never communicate the message of Jesus any way other than the plain method he used (nothing clever, articulate, or eloquent)? Explain your answer. (page 31)
- Read Acts 18:1-11. What additional insights do you gain from this passage about why Paul chose a simple approach to preaching the gospel to the Gentiles? (page 32)
- Read Isaiah 64:1-4 and 1 Corinthians 2:9. What glimpses of God's goodness can you identify in the midst of your "crazy" life?

Day 5: A Spiritual Mind

- Read 1 Corinthians 2:10-16. How would you summarize in one sentence what Paul is trying to tell us about God's Holy Spirit? (page 36)

- Read John 14:16-17. What are some of the ways the Holy Spirit helps us live godly lives (from this verse and any others that come to mind)?
- Paul said the Holy Spirit shows us God's deep secrets (1 Corinthians 2:10). What are some ways the Holy Spirit has revealed things to you personally? (page 38)
- Read Philippians 2:5-8 and 1 Corinthians 2:16. How does knowing that you possess the mind of Christ influence or affect your thought life?
- Allow women who completed the Weekly Wrap-up to briefly share any insights they gained from reading 1 Corinthians 1 and 2 in one sitting and reviewing highlights from the week's study.

Optional Group Activity (for a session longer than sixty minutes)

Pass out paper and pens or pencils (as needed), and ask the women to break into groups of three to five and compile a "top five" list of the qualities of a good leader. After a few minutes, come back together and have each group share their list. Ask: *What were some common threads in the lists? What different qualities were listed as number one?*

Say that some of us value certain characteristics in a leader over other qualities, and suggest that a helpful leadership acronym is FAT:

Faithful
Available
Teachable

Briefly discuss why these are important leadership qualities. Ask: *Which do you believe is more important: ability or humility? Why?*

Now break into your small groups again and list the top five qualities of a good follower. After a few minutes, come back together and ask: *What characteristics did your two lists have in common? What different characteristics did you identify?*

Read aloud or paraphrase:

> *At times, all of us are leaders; in other situations, we are followers. Paul reminds us in 1 Corinthians 1 and 2 not to get caught up focusing on the messenger. Instead, our focus should be on Christ alone and His gospel message.*

Prayer Requests

Before sharing prayer requests, take time for a brief announcement if you will be doing the Optional Group Activity in your next group session. Ask each woman to bring a picture from her childhood to your next session to share with the group. (Digital pictures on phones or tablets will work, but prints that can be passed around are preferable.)

Invite the group members to share prayer requests and pray for one another. Use index cards or sticky notes, popcorn prayer, or another prayer technique included in Tips for Tackling Five Common Challenges (pages 12-16) to lead this time with intentionality and sensitivity.

DIGGING DEEPER
WEEK 1 HIGHLIGHTS

My Town

See AbingdonPress.com/FirstCorinthians for the full article.

The places where we live shape us in ways we may not even realize. I grew up in a small town in East Texas. Even though I haven't lived in that town in over two decades, it shaped who I am today in many ways. For the original audience of Paul's First Letter to the Corinthians, their town had an impact on them as well. By learning a little about the geography, history, religion, and customs of Corinth, we can discover how the town shaped the Corinthian believers.

Geography

Corinth was located on "the four-and-one-half-mile (5,950-meter) Isthmus that bridged the Peloponnese and the mainland."[1] Many ships docked on one side of the Isthmus and carried their cargo overland through Corinth to another ship waiting on the other side; this saved going around the Peloponnese (peninsula). This made Corinth a commercial center for people of many different nationalities, offering a variety of pleasures for sale.

History

Corinth had flourished as a Greek city-state but then came into conflict with Rome and was destroyed by the Roman consul Lucius Mummius in 146 b.c. For 100 years Corinth was uninhabited until Julius Caesar rebuilt the city in 44 b.c.[2] Commentator Gordon Fee notes two reasons the city might have been rebuilt:

1. Corinth's strategic location for commerce gave it the potential for economic boom. It had water, harbors, and "control of the Isthmian games, which ranked just below the Olympian in importance."
2. Freedmen from Rome, whose status was just above that of slaves, repopulated the city of Corinth. Establishing a city in Corinth gave them an opportunity for advancement and eliminated potential trouble that might have been caused by their overabundance in Rome.[3]

Corinth was rebuilt by ambitious people looking for a fresh start. Within fifty years, the city was thriving economically. Fee notes, "Since money attracts people…, Corinth quickly experienced a great influx of people from both West and East, along with all the attendant gains and ills of such growth."[4] Along with economic concerns came moral difficulties. Not everyone enjoyed instant wealth. A large population of slaves and artisans made up a significant percentage of the people of Corinth.

Religion

Expression of religion in Corinth was as varied as the city's population. It is said that at least twenty-six sacred places existed in Corinth. While Corinth had a Jewish synagogue, Jews were a minority of the population of the city. Christians also made up a small fraction of the population. They were surrounded by neighbors, friends, and coworkers who ascribed to a melting pot of religious beliefs.

Customs

Imagine this scene as if Corinth is "your town": Open markets offer all sorts of wares to citizens and visitors. The Isthmian games (second only to the Olympics) bring in crowds seeking food, shelter, and souvenirs. Philosophers gather in the town square to discuss old and new ideas about the meaning of life. Different groups congregate at sacred places to worship a garden variety of gods. Family gatherings and business meetings take place in local temples that serve as a sort of open-air banquet hall or restaurant. Dock workers, soldiers, tentmakers, merchants, religious leaders, prostitutes, slaves, community leaders, and *nouveau riche* (new rich) business owners can be seen throughout the community. How do you think the town impacted the Corinthian believers' newfound faith in Jesus? How have the places you've lived shaped you? Some of the influences of our towns are beneficial; others can rot our souls if we do not allow God's Word to transform us. As we dig deep into 1 Corinthians, we will need to unwrap the culture of the original audience to see God's overriding principles. This will mean remembering what Corinth was like to the recipients of Paul's letter and asking God to help us see how our own towns have influenced us.

---

[1] Gordon Fee, *The New International Commentary on the New Testament: The First Epistle to the Corinthians, Revised Edition* (Grand Rapids: Eerdmans, 2014), 1.

[2] Ibid., 1-2.

[3] Ibid., 3.

[4] Ibid.

Week 2

GROWING UP

1 Corinthians 3–5

Leader Prep

Memory Verse

The Kingdom of God is not just a lot of talk; it is living by God's power. (1 Corinthians 4:20)

Digging Deeper

Read Digging Deeper Week 2, "Unstuck," and note any interesting facts or insights that you would like to share with the group. (See pages 32-33 for highlights; read the full article online at AbingdonPress.com/FirstCorinthians.)

Materials Needed

- *First Corinthians* DVD and DVD player
- Stick-on nametags and markers (optional)
- Index cards or sticky notes (optional—Scriptures and Prayer Requests)
- E-mail group members several days before the group session to remind each woman to bring a picture from her childhood to share with the group. Digital pictures on phones or tablets will work, but prints that can be passed around are preferable. (Optional Group Activity)

Session Outline

Note: Refer to the format templates on page 7 for suggested time allotments.

Welcome

Offer a word of welcome to the group. If time allows and you choose to provide food, invite the women to enjoy refreshments and fellowship. (Groups meeting for sixty minutes may want to have a time for food and fellowship before the official start time.) Be sure to watch the clock and move to the All Play icebreaker at the appropriate time.

All Play

Ask each group member to respond briefly to this question: *What is a favorite meal you like to eat—especially when someone else is preparing it?*

Read aloud or paraphrase:

> *Intending to eat healthy food but desiring unhealthy food that tastes good is a daily battle for many of us. Similarly, we long to study God's Word and pray more often than we do, but we struggle against our appetites for soul junk food. This week we've seen that Paul admonished the believers in Corinth to grow up spiritually through a progressing spiritual diet. Like them, we must evaluate how we are eating spiritually speaking. God longs for us to grow in faith so that we can be closer to Him and fulfill the mission He gave us in telling others about His love.*

Digging Deeper Insights

Share insights from Digging Deeper Week 2, "Unstuck" (highlights on pages 32-33; full article at AbingdonPress.com/FirstCorinthians). You might summarize the markers of growth and then ask: *Which marker stands out as more relevant in your life right now?* If you choose, encourage group members to read the full article online.

Prayer

Before playing the video segment, ask God to prepare the group to receive His Word and to hear His voice.

Video

Play the video for Week 2. Invite participants to complete the Video Viewer Guide for Week 2 in the participant book as they watch (pages 76-77). (Answers are provided on page 64 of this book.)

Group Discussion

Video Discussion Questions

- Which of the five markers of spiritual growth resonates most with you right now, and why? (a progressing spiritual diet, getting along with others, building a life with eternity in mind, an attitude of humility, living by God's power)
- What does spiritual diet have to do with spiritual growth? What can help us progress in our spiritual diet when we get "stuck"?
- What do getting along with others and having an attitude of humility have in common? What role does the Holy Spirit play in each?
- Why is the way that we spend our time, talents, and resources important?
- What is the difference between being challenged and being changed?

Participant Book Discussion Questions

Note: Page references are provided for those questions that relate to specific questions or activities in the participant book.

Before you begin, invite volunteers to look up the following Scriptures and be prepared to read them aloud when called upon. You might want to write each of the Scripture references on a separate index card or sticky note that you can hand out.

Scriptures: 1 Corinthians 3:3; James 4:1-3; 1 Corinthians 3:1-9; Psalm 141:5; 1 Corinthians 3:10-15; Matthew 7:24-27; John 5:39; Acts 4:11-12; Revelation 22:12; 1 Corinthians 4:1-7; Luke 12:42-43; 1 Corinthians 4:5; Romans 14:4; 1 Corinthians 4:20; 1 Corinthians 5:1-8; Matthew 16:5-12; 1 Corinthians 5:2; Galatians 6:1-2; 1 Corinthians 5:9-13; 2 Corinthians 2:4-11; Hebrews 13:17

Day 1: Words of Warning

- Read 1 Corinthians 3:3 and James 4:1-3. What themes do these passages have in common? Describe a time when someone spoke words you needed to hear—even if you didn't appreciate them initially. (page 47)
- Read 1 Corinthians 3:1-9. When giving a word of warning, what are some practical ways we can seek to be more loving so that we don't come across as shaming or judging? (Consider specifics related to timing, method, tone, and so on.) (page 48)
- Read Psalm 141:5. Why is accepting criticism so difficult? What guidelines for receiving criticism might you add to the ones given on page 49?

Day 2: Fireproof

- Read 1 Corinthians 3:10-15. What illustration did Paul use to describe the Christian life?
- Read Matthew 7:24-27, John 5:39, and Acts 4:11-12. Why is the foundation so critical?

- How does recognizing that Christ is the firm foundation for all believers affect your thinking about our differences? (page 53)
- Read Revelation 22:12. Knowing that when Christ returns we will stand together at a rewards judgment, how does that motivate you to spend your time, talent, and treasure differently? (page 54)
- What were some combustible and fireproof materials that you listed on page 56?
- What is one small change that would help you build with quality materials in your spiritual life this week? (page 57)

Day 3: Less Talk, More Action

- Read 1 Corinthians 4:1-7. The first point in the lesson for Day 3 is that "less talk, more action" means being a servant. How does serving others help keep us from being prideful?
- Read Luke 12:42-43. How does our Lord describe a faithful servant? (page 60)
- In which of the four areas listed on page 60 do you sense God calling you to make the most significant stewardship changes? (Health, Finances, Time management, Talents)
- Read 1 Corinthians 4:5 and Romans 14:4. Why are we to keep our focus on our own service rather than the decisions of others? (page 61)
- Read 1 Corinthians 4:20. In what ways does this verse convict and inspire you? (page 64)

Day 4: Good Judgment

- Read 1 Corinthians 5:1-8. Why do you think Paul is judging here when in the last chapter he told the believers not to judge?
- Read Matthew 16:5-12 and summarize what Jesus was cautioning the disciples about. (page 68)
- Read 1 Corinthians 5:2. What does Paul say our posture toward sin in the church should be? Now read Galatians 6:1-2. What posture should we take when we help someone back on the right path? (page 69)
- What new insights have you gained about good judgment? (page 70)

Day 5: Restoration

- Read 1 Corinthians 5:9-13. Ask for responses to the questions on page 71: Who should the church never judge? (v. 12) Who will judge them? (v. 13) Whom did Paul say the church is responsible to judge? (v. 12) How did Paul say they should deal with those in the church who were sinning? (v. 13)
- Read 2 Corinthians 2:4-11. What have you learned about the positive benefits that can come from properly carrying out loving church discipline? (page 73)
- Read Hebrews 13:17. What is the responsibility of your spiritual leaders? What are some practical ways we can give them reason to watch over us with joy instead of sorrow? (page 74)

- Allow women who completed the Weekly Wrap-up to briefly share any insights they gained from reading 1 Corinthians 3–5 in one sitting and reviewing highlights from the week's study.

Optional Group Activity (for a session longer than 60 minutes)

Ask the women to take out the childhood pictures they brought with them. (Digital pictures on phones will work, but prints that can be passed around are preferable.) If you have a large group (more than twelve), break into small groups of three to four for this activity. Have each participant pass around her picture as she tells something significant she remembers about her childhood at the time the picture was taken. Explain that the focus here is on the experience of growing up physically. This is not a time for women to go into great detail; instead, ask each woman to limit her sharing.

Now transition into a discussion of spiritual growth. You might begin by saying that while doctors can document increases in height and weight on a growth chart, spiritual growth can be much more difficult to track. Just as we have physical growth spurts, so we often have spiritual growth spurts. (My son grew seven inches in the eighth grade; it was an intense growth spurt for him!) Many of us have encountered trials or attended conferences or retreats that have accompanied seasons of intense spiritual growth for us.

Invite the women to share about a spiritual growth spurt they've experienced—a time when they began feeding themselves spiritual food, serving others, or transitioning from being more self-centered to being more others-focused.

Prayer Requests

End by inviting the group members to share prayer requests and pray for one another. Use index cards or sticky notes, popcorn prayer, or another prayer technique included in Tips for Tackling Five Common Challenges (pages 12-16) to lead this time with intentionality and sensitivity.

DIGGING DEEPER
WEEK 2 HIGHLIGHTS

Unstuck

See AbingdonPress.com/FirstCorinthians for the full article.

Spiritually speaking, we can get stuck when our walk with the Lord becomes stagnant. Some Christians remain in spiritual infancy like a baby wanting to be bottle-fed, rather than growing and learning to feed themselves. Other Christians do not move past childhood, expecting others to care for their spiritual needs. Yet in 1 Corinthians, Paul calls the church to grow up to feed themselves and even prepare spiritual food for others. As we consider how to get "unstuck," we must ask the question *What helps people grow?* In their book *How People Grow*, John Townsend and Henry Cloud identify some key concepts that can help us grow personally as well as equip us to encourage others to get unstuck in their spiritual lives. Here are summaries of a few highlights.[1]

Time. Spiritual growth doesn't happen overnight. God uses time as one way to grow his people.

Recognizing Our Need. Most people begin to grow when they recognize a need—whether for God or for growth—or they have a problem that they cannot solve on their own.

Relationships. According to Townsend and Cloud, "Spiritual growth doesn't occur in a vacuum. It happens within intimate, vulnerable relationships with God and safe people."[2]

Identification of Issues. Sometimes as Christians we try a one-size-fits-all program to help people grow. However, our creative God made us different. By looking for underlying issues and recognizing that we aren't all the same, we can help each other grow.

Ownership. We must take personal responsibility in order to grow, learning to differentiate our own mistakes from the past, the flaws of others, and the parts of life that are just the result of living in a broken world. Blaming people and circumstances will prevent us from moving forward.

Practicing New Behaviors. This is where we implement new methods that help us go deeper in faith. If we want to experience growth, we must practice new behaviors.

Forgiveness and Grief. Lifting up pain to God helps us grow. We get unstuck when we acknowledge wrongs that have been done to us and suffering that we have endured and then allow God to heal our brokenness.

Real Change. If we are truly growing in our faith, then our relationship with the Lord should be different today that it was last year. Townsend and Cloud observe, "As the inside grows, so ultimately should the outside."[3]

Maturity. We should never stop growing but should "go deeper..., bringing more and more to the light of God's healing grace."[4] New areas of growth will always come to light, and we should see steady progress toward intimacy with Jesus as we pursue movement out of our stuck places.

As you reflect on these markers of spiritual growth, does one stand out as being more relevant in your life right now? Is there a change God is calling you to make so that you can get unstuck and grow in your faith?

---

[1] Henry Cloud and John Townsend, *How People Grow: What the Bible Reveals about Personal Growth* (Grand Rapids: Zondervan, 2001), 357-60.

[2] Ibid. 358.

[3] Ibid. 360.

[4] Ibid. 360.

Week 3

EVERYBODY'S DOING IT

1 Corinthians 6–8

Leader Prep

Memory Verse

But you must be careful so that your freedom does not cause others with a weaker conscience to stumble. (1 Corinthians 8:9)

Digging Deeper

Read Digging Deeper Week 3, "Defining Church," and note any interesting facts or insights you would like to share with the group. (See pages 39-40 for highlights; read the full article online at AbingdonPress.com/FirstCorinthians.)

Materials Needed

- *First Corinthians* DVD and DVD player
- Stick-on nametags and markers (optional)
- Index cards or sticky notes (optional—Scriptures and Prayer Requests)

Session Outline

Note: Refer to the format templates on page 7 for suggested time allotments.

Welcome

Offer a word of welcome to the group. If time allows and you choose to provide food, invite the women to enjoy refreshments and fellowship. (Groups meeting for sixty minutes may want to have a time for food and fellowship before the official start time.) Be sure to watch the clock and move to the All Play icebreaker at the appropriate time.

All Play

Ask each group member to respond briefly to this question: *What is the last piece of technology you acquired—fitness tracker, phone, tablet, laptop, television, other—whether you purchased it or it was a gift?*

Read aloud or paraphrase:

> *While technology and culture are ever changing, God and His principles remain the same. Our culture may differ greatly from that of the original audience of Paul's first letter to the Corinthians, but like them we struggle to follow God in a culture that lives for selfish pleasure. We need discernment to know which aspects of culture are okay and which might lead us into sin. This was challenging for the church at Corinth, and it's difficult for us as well. We live under grace, not law, but we seek to live in a way that honors Jesus. Sorting this out requires constant evaluation of what we are doing and why we are doing it.*

Digging Deeper Insights

Share insights from Digging Deeper Week 3, "Defining Church" (highlights on pages 39-40; full article at AbingdonPress.com/FirstCorinthians). You might share the qualities or markers of a church (as opposed to a gathering of Christ-followers) and then ask: *What does it mean to approach the church as servants of Christ rather than consumers?* If you choose, encourage group members to read the full article online.

Prayer

Before playing the video segment, ask God to prepare the group to receive His Word and to hear His voice.

Video

Play the video for Week 3. Invite participants to complete the Video Viewer Guide for Week 3 in the participant book as they watch (pages 106–107).(Answers are provided on page 64 of this book.)

Group Discussion

Video Discussion Questions

- What helps you follow Jesus even when the winds of culture are blowing in a totally different direction?
- How can we keep from comforting ourselves or escaping with worldly things rather than turning to Jesus—especially when everybody else seems to be doing it?
- What does honoring God with our bodies involve? How does this affect our spiritual condition?
- Review the three questions we can ask ourselves when making decisions related to God's permissive will (see the Video Viewer Guide, pages 106–107). Choose one area where God may lead us to make different decisions, and discuss how these questions can help us discern God's best for us in our particular situation.

Participant Book Discussion Questions

Note: Page references are provided for those questions that relate to specific questions or activities in the participant book.

Before you begin, invite volunteers to look up the following Scriptures and be prepared to read them aloud when called upon. You might want to write each of the Scripture references on a separate index card or sticky note that you can hand out.

Scriptures: 1 Corinthians 6:1-8; Romans 13:1-5; Proverbs 13:8; Matthew 5:39-41; 1 Corinthians 6:9-11; 1 Corinthians 6:12-17; Galatians 5:13; Romans 6:1-4; 1 Corinthians 6:18-20; 1 Corinthians 8:1-3; 1 Corinthians 8:9-13; Matthew 18:1-7

Day 1: Standing Against Injustice

- Read 1 Corinthians 6:1-8 and summarize one or two principles that stand out to you. (page 80) Now read Romans 13:1-5. Drawing from both passages, what are some guiding directives for a Christian's involvement in civil lawsuits, and for secular government's involvement in criminal affairs?
- Read Proverbs 13:8. What are some practical ways God might be calling you to stand up for injustice—whether across the globe, right in your own community, or anywhere in between? (page 82)
- Read Matthew 5:39-41. Consider a conflict you might be involved in right now—with a family member, church member, coworker, neighbor, or friend. How might Jesus be calling you to follow Him by giving up your rights? (page 83)

Day 2: Sex

- Read 1 Corinthians 6:9-11. What do we learn about the past lives of some of the Corinthian believers from verses 9-11? According to verse 11, what made the change in their lives? (page 85)

- Read 1 Corinthians 6:12-17, Galatians 5:13, and Romans 6:1-4. How did you summarize what these passages are teaching? (page 86)
- Read 1 Corinthians 6:18-20. What instructions do we find here regarding sexual sin? (Refer to the chart on page 88.)
- Discuss the two principles or insights that stood out to you from today's lesson as recorded on page 89.

Day 3: Preferences and Absolutes

- Ask group members to glance back over 1 Corinthians 7, and remind them that on Day 3 we looked at the difference between God's prescriptive and permissive will. What are some commands from Scripture that you would categorize as prescriptive—instructions that are true for every believer? (page 92) What are some issues about which you have made decisions according to God's permissive will? These are things that are right for you but may not be right for others. (page 92)
- What potential dangers are there for the Christian community when we turn permissive principles into prescriptive ones that we enforce on all believers?
- What stood out to you from this day of study?

Day 4: Information Overload

- In what ways have you experienced information overload? (page 95)
- Read 1 Corinthians 8:1-3. Like the Corinthians, we live in a culture where knowledge is considered power. How do these verses encourage or convict you personally? (page 96)
- What comes to mind when you think of areas where we disagree about how to apply our freedom in Christ? Think of choices or decisions that might be acceptable for one person but considered to be sin for another in light of her or his past. (page 98)
- How do you discern between biblical truth that should not be compromised and issues of conscience? (page 98)

Day 5: Liberty and Love

- How have you seen relationships among believers affected by a disagreement over a gray area or conscience issue? (page 101)
- Read 1 Corinthians 8:9-13. What principles can we apply from these verses? (Refer to the exercise on pages 101–102.)
- Read Matthew 18:1-7. What additional insights related to how our decisions affect others do we glean from these words of Jesus?
- Allow women who completed the Weekly Wrap-up to briefly share any insights they gained from reading 1 Corinthians 6–8 in one sitting and reviewing highlights from the week's study.

Optional Group Activity (for a session longer than sixty minutes)

Ask two volunteers to come forward and stand with their backs to each other. Ask the other group members to call out things about these two volunteers that are different. As each difference is called, the volunteers are to take one step apart. When they reach the end of the available space, have them turn and face each other. Now, ask the audience to call out similarities of the volunteers. As each similarity is called out, the volunteers are to take one step toward each other. Conclude by saying something like this: *Differences can divide us, while focusing on what we have in common brings us closer together.*

Discuss:

- Think about the things that were noted as differences. How many were things that we can easily see (size, hair color, skin color, clothing, and so on)?
- What were some of the similarities?

Note that while some physical characteristics may be similar, many other characteristics are not as visible. For example, both women may be outgoing or have similar hobbies.

Now ask each person to turn to the person next to her and find one similarity and one difference they have. As time allows, let the pairs report their findings.

Read or summarize:

This week in 1 Corinthians 6–8 we found that differences can lead to disagreement. While our issue probably isn't eating meat sacrificed to idols as it was for the Corinthian believers, we do find that differences in our background, appearance, culture, or theology can cause arguments. We can look for common ground with people who seem very different from us. By looking for and focusing on similarities, we then are able to dialogue better when we disagree.

Prayer Requests

End by inviting the group members to share prayer requests and pray for one another. Use index cards or sticky notes, popcorn prayer, or another prayer technique included in Tips for Tackling Five Common Challenges (pages 12-16) to lead this time with intentionality and sensitivity.

DIGGING DEEPER
WEEK 3 HIGHLIGHTS
Defining Church

See AbingdonPress.com/FirstCorinthians for the full article.

In order to define what church is, we must first define what it is not.

The church is not a building. The early Christians met in homes, gathering in groups of around thirty to fifty people.

The church is not an event. The church is much more than a worship service. According to 1 Corinthians, the church was to do things that would strengthen everyone present, such as sing, teach, and share revelations from God. In 1 Corinthians 16:2 we learn that they were to set aside a portion of their money on the first day of each week for an offering. These are not prescriptive passages, mandating that all church gatherings must include these elements; rather, they are descriptive passages, conveying some of the things that occurred when a body of believers met as a church.

The church is not a business. It is true that local churches must manage their staff and budgets, but a church is meant to be a living organism rather than an organization. Paul used the human body as an analogy of how the church is to function (see Romans 12:4-5 and 1 Corinthians 12:11, 18, 27). The church is also called the bride of Christ (2 Corinthians 11:2; Ephesians 5:25-32).

So, what exactly is a church? The Greek word he used is *ekklesia*, which means "a gathering of citizens called out from their homes into some public place, an assembly."[1] Theologians refer to the study of the church as ecclesiology. So, the church refers to people. Historically, the church was seen as beginning with the Apostle Peter and continuing in apostolic succession (being transmitted from the apostles through successive church leaders)—with the church viewed as the gatekeeper of grace and truth. After the Protestant Reformation in the sixteenth century, the church splintered into denominational factions with distinct labels. In the modern church era there is a movement among some branches of the church away from historical roots and labels of ecclesiology.

Labels used to inform ecclesiology. In other words, we used to know the gist of a congregation's beliefs and practice based on the denominational label. Though that is still true in a general sense, today we are seeing more diversity of practice and belief among churches within the same denomination. Many churches have dropped or moved away from denominational labels to allow for more flexibility and foster a generic impression. The idea is not to mislead people or even to

Week 3

abandon denominational affiliations—though some have done so—but to emphasize our common faith foundation rather than our distinctions. Without a label, ecclesiology cannot be as easily ascertained.

Jesus said in Matthew 18:20, "For where two or three gather together as my followers, I am there among them." However, as we look at the whole of Scripture, we see that although Jesus is there when two or three gather, not every gathering of two or three is a church meeting. We must remember that when the word *ekklesia* is used in Scripture, it can refer to two different things:

- **The church universal** – this includes all Christ followers across the planet. Scripture employs the metaphors of a bride and body to illustrate the church's relationship to Christ. Both are living organisms rather than organizations. (See 2 Corinthians 11:2; 15:9; Ephesians 1:22-23; Colossians 1:18)
- **The local church** – this includes local bodies of believers. Through Paul's letters to various churches we find local bodies of believers had leadership, structure, and regular gatherings. (See 1 Thessalonians 1:1; 1 Corinthians 4:17; 2 Corinthians 11:8)

So what delineates an actual church, as opposed to a group of Christ-followers who assemble together? We find some marks that distinguish the church in Scripture. Though scholars have differing opinions, some common threads include the following:

- **Community expressions of worship** – singing, giving, serving one another with spiritual gifts, etc. (1 Corinthians 12:7, 14:15; 2 Corinthians 8:3-7; Ephesians 5:19; Colossians 3:16)
- **Preaching and teaching of the Word of God** (Acts 2:14-41, 13:16-47; 1 Corinthians 14:4)
- **Biblical leadership** (Acts 14:23; 1 Timothy 3:1-7, 4:14, 5:17; Titus 1:5-9; James 5:14)
- **The practice of sacraments/ordinances** – Lord's Supper/Baptism (Acts 2:37-40; 1 Corinthians 11:17-34)
- **An accountable community** – church discipline, providing for those with needs (Matthew 18:15-17; Acts 6:1-4; Romans 15:26; 1 Corinthians 5:1-13; 2 Thessalonians 3:6-15)
- **Discipleship processes to help people mature in faith** (1 Corinthians 4:16, 11:1; Ephesians 4:15; Philippians 4:9; Hebrews 13:7; 2 Peter 1:8-10, 3:18)
- **A gospel mission to help others hear God's message** (Matthew 28:18-20)

As we seek to understand who we are as part of God's church, we realize that God has called us to assemble with others to fulfill His mission. God calls us to come together for worship and teaching not only for our own benefit, but also so that we can serve others.

---

[1] *Ekklesia*, Strong's Concordance1577, http://www.biblestudytools.com/lexicons /greek/kjv/ekklesia.html.

Week 4

Beyond Ourselves
1 Corinthians 9–11

Leader Prep

Memory Verses

When I am with those who are weak, I share their weakness, for I want to bring the weak to Christ. Yes, I try to find common ground with everyone, doing everything I can to save some. I do everything to spread the Good News and share in its blessings. (1 Corinthians 9:22-23)

Digging Deeper

Read Digging Deeper Week 4, "Loving Boundaries," and note any interesting facts or insights you would like to share with the group. (See pages 46-47 for highlights; read the full article at AbingdonPress.com/FirstCorinthians.)

Materials Needed

- *First Corinthians* DVD and DVD player
- Stick-on nametags and markers (optional)
- Index cards or sticky notes (optional—Scriptures and Prayer Requests)
- Twenty items (household items, knickknacks, toiletries, and so on), tray or platter, cloth to cover tray and items, whiteboard (or posterboard), eraser, markers (Optional Group Activity)

Session Outline

Note: Refer to the format templates on page 7 for suggested time allotments.

Welcome

Offer a word of welcome to the group. If time allows and you choose to provide food, invite the women to enjoy refreshments and fellowship. (Groups meeting for sixty minutes may want to have a time for food and fellowship before the official start time.) Be sure to watch the clock and move to the All Play icebreaker at the appropriate time.

All Play

Ask each group member to respond briefly to this question: *How do you like to order/ make your favorite hot drink?*

Read aloud or paraphrase:

> *Getting beyond ourselves means allowing God to fill us up with His love so we can pour it out on others. This week we found selfishness at the root of many of the problems the church in Corinth was experiencing. We certainly can relate to their plight. Our world tells us to make personal happiness our first priority. In Jesus' reverse economy, we find Him calling us to put Him first and expend our lives for the sake of others. This is the true path to joy.*

Digging Deeper Insights

Share insights from Digging Deeper Week 4, "Loving Boundaries" (highlights on pages 46-47; full article at AbingdonPress.com/FirstCorinthians). Consider sharing the warning signs of behavior that is less loving than we might think. Then ask this question: *What helps you determine what the most loving response is in a particular situation?* If you choose, encourage group members to read the full article online.

Prayer

Before playing the video segment, ask God to prepare the group to receive His Word and to hear His voice.

Video

Play the video for Week 4. Invite participants to complete the Video Viewer Guide for Week 4 in the participant book as they watch (page 141). (Answers are provided on page 64 of this book.)

Group Discussion

Video Discussion Questions

- What does it mean to "get beyond ourselves" and "give up our rights" when it comes to sharing the gospel? Why is this important?
- Who have been some of the "agents of love" in your life—people who have walked with you and have been the hands and feet of Christ?
- How have you found common ground with others in order to share the gospel?
- Why do we need a spiritual training plan? What happens when we neglect our spiritual health?

Participant Book Discussion Questions

Note: Page references are provided for those questions that relate to specific questions or activities in the participant book.

Before you begin, invite volunteers to look up the following Scriptures and be prepared to read them aloud when called upon. You might want to write each of the Scripture references on a separate index card or sticky note that you can hand out.

Scriptures: 1 Corinthians 9:15-21; 1 Corinthians 9:22-23; 1 Corinthians 9:24-27; 1 Corinthians 10:1-5; 1 Corinthians 10:6-11; Colossians 3:5; 1 Corinthians 10:12-13; 1 Corinthians 10:23-24; 1 Corinthians 10:31-33; 1 Corinthians 11:1-16; John 10:30; John 14:28; Luke 22:14-20; 1 Corinthians 11:17-34

Day 1: So Worth It

- Paul went to great lengths to convince the church at Corinth that he had valid rights. Glance over 1 Corinthians 9:1-14. What were some of Paul's arguments for his right to be paid?
- Read 1 Corinthians 9:15-21. What things have you given up, or what personal inconveniences have you chosen, in order to share God's message with others—through words and/or service? (page 112)
- Read 1 Corinthians 9:22-23. What are some practical ways you can look for common ground with someone you know who does not follow Christ? (page 113)
- Read 1 Corinthians 9:24-27. What spiritual disciplines do you regularly practice to stay strong spiritually? How have these spiritual disciplines impacted your spiritual growth in the last year? (page 116)

Day 2: Caution Signs

- Read 1 Corinthians 10:1-5. What were the three caution signs Paul mentioned in these verses that we focused on in Day 2?
- Read 1 Corinthians 10:6-11. What reason did Paul give for this history lesson? (page 119)

- Read Colossians 3:5. How would you describe the difference between a day when your personal idols keep you focused inward and a day when your resolve to put God first gives you an outward focus? (Think about what is different in your thought life, attitude, words, and actions.) (page 120)
- How would you define the word *contentment*? (page 122) Describe an area in your life where you are struggling to embrace contentment.
- Read 1 Corinthians 10:12-13. How do these verses encourage you in your spiritual life?

Day 3: Offended

- Read 1 Corinthians 10:23-24. Now turn to page 125. Consider the decisions you have made in some of the gray areas included in the bulleted list. What helped you discern your personal position?
- Ask if anyone might be willing to share one of the situations she wrote in the chart at the bottom of page 127.
- Read 1 Corinthians 10:31-33. How did you summarize these verses on page 128? What two questions did we identify from these verses that can help us discern how to proceed in a gray area? How did these questions help you determine what to do in a gray area in your life? What will glorify the Lord in this situation? (Refer to your responses on page 128.)

Day 4: Interdependent

- Read 1 Corinthians 11:1-16. What questions or comments did these verses bring to mind? (page 129)
- Read John 10:30 and John 14:28. What do we learn from these verses about the relationship between Jesus and the Father? How is God calling you to embrace humility in a relationship of subordination or willing submission—whether at work or church, in a volunteer organization, or in a family situation? (page 133)
- Review the three principles regarding the passage about head coverings. What questions or issues do these three principles raise for you? (page 134)
- Which one of the three principles stands out most to you right now, and why? (page 134)

Day 5: Remembering Together

- Read Luke 22:14-20. According to verse 19, why did Jesus say we should take the cup and the bread? (page 136)
- Read 1 Corinthians 11:17-34. What two things did Paul encourage the Corinthians to do in verses 28 and 33? (page 138)
- How do these truths from God's Word challenge you in your attitude toward the Lord's Supper? (page 138)
- Allow women who completed the Weekly Wrap-up to briefly share any insights they gained from reading 1 Corinthians 9–11 in one sitting and reviewing highlights from the week's study.

Optional Group Activity (for a session longer than sixty minutes)

Bring out the tray of twenty items covered with a cloth (household items, knickknacks, toiletries, and so on). Allow the women to look at the tray for thirty seconds, and then cover it again. Say,

Usually this game is used as a competition to see who can remember the most items on the tray. Instead, we are going to remember together. Let's work together and see how many items we can remember.

As the women call out the items they remember, write them on a posterboard or whiteboard. When they cannot remember any more of the items, ask: *Do you think you would have been able to remember all of these items by yourself?* (Pause for responses.) *When it comes to our faith, what are some practical ways we can encourage each other with God's truth regularly?* As the women share ideas, write them on the whiteboard or the other side of the posterboard. (Ideas: text verses of encouragement, send messages or cards letting others know we are praying for them, regularly attend church services or Bible study with others, serve together, and so on.) Encourage participants to choose one of these ways to get beyond themselves and encourage others this week.

Prayer Requests

End by inviting the group members to share prayer requests and pray for one another. Use index cards or sticky notes, popcorn prayer, or another prayer technique included in "Tips for Tackling Five Common Challenges" (pages 12-16) to lead this time with intentionality and sensitivity.

DIGGING DEEPER WEEK 4 HIGHLIGHTS

Loving Boundaries

See AbingdonPress.com/FirstCorinthians for the full article.

Knowing when love should say–"yes"–and when it should say–"no"–can be a fine line to walk, especially in difficult relationships. The Holy Spirit and good counselors are our allies when it comes to discerning when relationships need a loving boundary. As Scripture tells us, "When the Spirit of truth comes, he will guide you into all truth. He will not speak on his own but will tell you what he has heard. He will tell you about the future" (John 16:13), and "Plans go wrong for lack of advice; / many advisers bring success" (Proverbs 15:22).

In her book *Can Christians Love Too Much?* Dr. Margaret J. Rinck offers a few warning signs that our behavior may not be as loving as we might think:[1]

- **Self-neglect.** Rinck writes, "We love others 'too much' when loving others causes us to chronically and severely neglect our own needs."[2] God calls us to rest and care for our own bodies so that we can serve Him and others. If we are loving others to the point that our own physical, spiritual, emotional, and mental needs are neglected, we must consider if we might have some unhealthy patterns in the name of "love."
- **Identity loss.** Another way we love "too much" is when we lose our identity in the relationship. In 1 Corinthians Paul compares the church to a body. We are to work together in harmony but retain our individual uniqueness. We must be careful to find our identity in who we are in Christ rather than in what we do for others.
- **Compulsion.** Loving because of fear or a sense that we "have to" is a sign that we are loving too much. If we love others because we are scared that we might be neglected, disliked, or hurt in some way, we can find ourselves always saying yes when we would like to say no. Authentic love is free to choose.

Though I believe that what Dr. Rinck is describing is not love in excess but rather a misplaced definition of love, I understand why she chose the phrase "love too much." As followers of Jesus, we serve a sacrificial and loving God. At times we can equate love with always giving others what they want.

However, real love gives people what they need rather than what they want. When it comes to children, for example, we know it is not loving to give them everything they want. If we did, they would be unhealthy and unhappy. Sometimes when my husband and

I disciplined our children, they would say, "You don't love me!" We were quick to affirm our love and point out this biblical truth: "Those who love their children care enough to discipline them" (Proverbs 13:24b).

It can be easier to give in, pretend we did not see bad behavior, or sacrifice our own needs in the name of love. However, we must ask ourselves, "What will actually be the most loving thing to do in this situation?" Love does not give an alcoholic a drink, cover up for a physically abusive spouse, or lie for our children. Often real love stands up for injustice, rejoices in the truth, and allows others to experience consequences so that they can grow. If you are in a situation where you question whether love has crossed the line into codependency, I encourage you to talk with a trained counselor or pastor in order to determine if setting a boundary might be the most loving thing to do.

---

[1] Dr. Margaret J. Rinck, *Can Christians Love Too Much: Breaking the Cycle of Codependency.* (Grand Rapids: Zondervan, 1990), 16–18.

[2] Ibid. 17.

Week 5

LIVING LOVE

1 Corinthians 12–14

Leader Prep

Memory Verse

Three things will last forever—faith, hope, and love—and the greatest of these is love.
(1 Corinthians 13:13)

Digging Deeper

Read the Digging Deeper Week 5 articles, "A Controversial Gift" and "The Sound of Silence," and note any interesting facts or insights you would like to share with the group. (See pages 53-56 for highlights; read the full articles at AbingdonPress.com /FirstCorinthians.)

Materials Needed

- *First Corinthians* DVD and DVD player
- Stick-on nametags and markers (optional)
- Index cards or sticky notes (optional—Scriptures and Prayer Requests)
- Two printed copies of a well-known painting, photograph, or other familiar image full of details (look for images online); scissors, white paper, markers, rulers, pens, and pencils for participants (Optional Group Activity)

Session Outline

Note: Refer to the format templates on page 7 for suggested time allotments.

Welcome

Offer a word of welcome to the group. If time allows and you choose to provide food, invite the women to enjoy refreshments and fellowship. (Groups meeting for sixty minutes may want to have a time for food and fellowship before the official start time.) Be sure to watch the clock and move to the All Play icebreaker at the appropriate time.

All Play

Ask each group member to respond briefly to this question: *What was your experience like the last time you worked on a puzzle—or if you haven't done that in a very long time, what is a game or hobby you enjoy?*

Read aloud or paraphrase:

> *Life can be puzzling at times. God calls us to show His love to others even when we don't understand all the pieces of our lives. The Corinthians were struggling with an issue related to spiritual gifts. They valued some more than others. It may not be spiritual gifts for us, but we can be prone to overfocus on one area and neglect others. While we strive for balance and seek to understand the bigger picture, God calls us to love His way—with patience and kindness, leaving behind record keeping, rudeness, and irritability. We need God's help to display these attributes as we sort out the pieces of our puzzling lives.*

Digging Deeper Insights

Share insights from the Digging Deeper Week 5 articles, "A Controversial Gift" and "The Sound of Silence" (highlights on pages 53-56; full articles at AbingdonPress.com /FirstCorinthians). You might summarize the three views regarding the gift of tongues and the three views regarding Paul's instruction for women to be silent in church. Then ask these questions: *How can cultural context help us interpret and apply these verses? What questions do these passages raise for you?* (Consider listing participants' questions on a board or chart and challenging the women to do their own study to find answers. If you like, you could have individuals choose from the questions and share findings at a future group session.) If you choose, encourage group members to read the full articles online.

Prayer

Before playing the video segment, ask God to prepare the group to receive His Word and to hear His voice.

Video

Play the video for Week 5. Invite participants to complete the Video Viewer Guide for Week 5 in the participant book as they watch (page 173). (Answers are provided on page 64 of this book.)

Group Discussion

Video Discussion Questions

- First Corinthians 13 gives us a picture of God's love. How would you describe what God's love looks like? How does receiving God's love help us love others?
- Is it more difficult for you to give or receive love? Why?
- Is it possible to love God without loving God's people? Explain your answer.
- Share a way that God has called you to love His people.
- Why is it important to love and support one another in conflict? How does remembering that our view is partial and incomplete help us do this?

Participant Book Discussion Questions

Note: Page references are provided for those questions that relate to specific questions or activities in the participant book.

Before you begin, invite volunteers to look up the following Scriptures and be prepared to read them aloud when called upon. You might want to write each of the Scripture references on a separate index card or sticky note that you can hand out.

Scriptures: Matthew 7:11; James 1:17; 1 Corinthians 12:1-11; Romans 12:6-8; Ephesians 4:11; 1 Peter 4:10-11; 1 Corinthians 12:12-31; 1 John 4:7-12; 1 Corinthians 13:1-3; 1 Corinthians 13:4-7; 1 Corinthians 13:8-13; Romans 10:17; 1 Corinthians 14:1-3; 1 Corinthians 14:7-11; 1 Corinthians 14:26-40; Isaiah 55:8-9; Psalm 85:8; Acts 10:36; Philippians 4:7; James 3:13-18

Day 1: Opening Presents

- Read Matthew 7:11 and James 1:17. What do we learn about God's gifts in each of these passages? (page 143)
- Read 1 Corinthians 12:1-11. In verses 4-6, Paul drives home an important principle concerning spiritual gifts. Summarize in one sentence what he was trying to communicate. (page 144)
- Read Romans 12:6-8, Ephesians 4:11, and 1 Peter 4:10-11. What additional insights did you glean from these passages regarding spiritual gifts? (page 145)
- Turn to page 146. As you look over the list of gifts, which two would you say might be gifts God has given you?

Day 2: Head, Shoulders, Knees, and Toes

- Read 1 Corinthians 12:12-31. What are some of the different backgrounds you see in your church and/or other church bodies in your area? (page 149)
- What are some disagreements or problems you have seen among believers because of differences? (page 149)
- How did you fill in the blanks for this sentence: "The Lord has given me the special ability to _____, and I will use this to help others by _____"? (page 151)
- What is one truth from today's lesson that stands out to you? (page 152)

Day 3: The Greatest of These

- Read 1 John 4:7-12. Share some insights you received from answering the questions related to these verses on page 153.
- Read 1 Corinthians 13:1-3. Which example Paul mentioned do you think would be most impressive to include on your resume? When and how have you experienced the truth that a lack of love drains the value from a possession, talent, gift, or relationship? (page 154)
- Read 1 Corinthians 13:4-7. As you consider God's call to love others with this kind of love, in what areas of your life do you sense God speaking a word of affirmation or encouragement? In what areas do you sense the conviction of the Holy Spirit? (page 156)
- Read 1 Corinthians 13:8-13. How does recognizing that your own knowledge is partial and incomplete motivate you to be more gracious toward someone you currently disagree with? (page 157)

Day 4: Pursuing Love in Real Life Situations

- Read Romans 10:17 and 1 Corinthians 14:1-3. What are three benefits of speaking prophecy in the church? (page 162)
- How have you seen a group or individual overconcentrate on one aspect of Christianity? Where in your faith or life do you lack balance right now? (page 162)
- Read 1 Corinthians 14:7-11. What are three ways Paul illustrated the need for intelligibility? (page 164)
- What is something God has been teaching you that you would like to share with one or more persons in your life (think kids, grandkids, neighbors, coworkers, friends, or people you disciple or mentor)? How can you share it in a way that will be relevant to this person or persons? (page 165)

Day 5: Solution-oriented

- Read 1 Corinthians 14:26-40. What is something we learn about God's character in verse 33? Does having things in order typically bring you peace? Why or why not? (page 166)

- Read Isaiah 55:8-9, Psalm 85:8, Acts 10:36, and Philippians 4:7. What did you learn about God in each of these verses? (page 167)
- Read James 3:13-18. According to these verses, what kind of forces are at the heart of disorder? (page 167)
- How have you seen a plan bring order to a church service, an organization, or a relationship? (page 168)
- Allow the women who completed the Weekly Wrap-up to briefly share any insights they gained from reading 1 Corinthians 12–14 in one sitting and reviewing highlights from the week's study.

Optional Group Activity (for a session longer than sixty minutes)

In advance, look online for a well-known image that is full of details, and print two copies. Cut one of the images into squares (if you have an even number of participants, cut equally sized squares totaling the number of participants in your group; if you have an odd number of participants, round up to the next even number). Hide the intact image until the second part of the activity.

Part 1 (allow about 5 minutes): Give each participant a piece of the puzzle without telling what it is. If you have an extra piece, ask someone to take two. Pass out paper, markers, pens, pencils, rulers, and scissors. Now instruct each participant to create an exact copy of the image of her puzzle piece on a blank sheet of printer paper. Regardless of artistic ability, each woman is to replicate on a larger scale the image that is on her puzzle piece. (If you have a larger group, you can cut fewer squares and have the women work in groups of two or three for each puzzle piece, rather than cutting a square for every person.) As they draw, the women will not know why or how their own work affects the larger picture.

Part 2 (allow about 5 minutes): When all have completed their enlargements, reveal the copy of the intact image and work together to assemble the pieces into a giant replica of the original (either on a large table or the floor). Remind the group that we do not have all the puzzle pieces, yet God sees how all the pieces will come together. When we see only a partial picture, it can be confusing. However, when we keep the bigger picture in mind, remembering that God has a sovereign plan for the pieces of our lives, we can love each other well through the process.

Prayer Requests

End by inviting the group members to share prayer requests and pray for one another. Use index cards or sticky notes, popcorn prayer, or another prayer technique included in "Tips for Tackling Five Common Challenges" (pages 12-16) to lead this time with intentionality and sensitivity.

DIGGING DEEPER WEEK 5 HIGHLIGHTS

A Controversial Gift

See AbingdonPress.com/FirstCorinthians for the full article.

So many factors shape our understanding of Scripture. Our religious upbringings and traditions, our exposure to different theological ideas and beliefs, and the views of those we respect can shape our reading of the Scriptures. Understandably, there are some passages and details that are highly disputed and debated among Christians.

The spiritual gift of tongues, which Paul references in chapters 12 and 14 of his First Letter to the Corinthians, is one example. Throughout church history there has been much controversy surrounding the gift of tongues, and not much has changed through the centuries in these disagreements. Today we still argue over what it means to speak in tongues, how this gift is to be used, and whether it is relevant in the modern era. There are essentially three major views, although there are variations of thought within them.

1. Cessationism. Those who hold this view believe the gift of tongues has ceased. People in this camp tend to associate the gift with the supernatural ability to speak authentic foreign languages. They believe that, as in Acts 2 when the people gathered on Pentecost heard the gospel in their own languages, the spiritual gift of tongues has to do with the ability to speak real languages rather than ecstatic utterances (unintelligible sounds). Some of the ideas within this view include the following:

- The early church fathers seemed to de-emphasize the gift of tongues. Irenaeus, Chrysostom, Augustine, and Tertullian wrote and taught extensively but gave little floor time to this spiritual gift.
- The gift of tongues related to actual foreign languages that God enabled people to speak. New Testament believers spoke a variety of languages. In Corinth there were people from many different places, such as Aquila and Priscilla who were deported from Italy to Corinth during a time of persecution of the Jews. Christians also faced persecution and moved often during the Diaspora—a time when the believers were scattered abroad.
- Some cessationists hold to a dispensational view, identifying God as working in different ways during different time periods. They believe the gift was active during what is called the Apostolic Age—when the gospel was authenticated through supernatural outward expressions such as tongues. Some cite 1 Corinthians 13:10,

which speaks of a time of perfection to come, as a reference to the finished canon of Scripture: "But when the time of perfection comes, these partial things will become useless." They believe that when the Bible was complete, "sign gifts" such as tongues were no longer needed; and so in the dispensation of the Church Age, in which we currently live, tongues are no longer in use. Some say that the decline of the gift of tongues in early church history supports this view.

2. Charismaticism. In this view, the gift of tongues is seen as a high-profile gift associated with what is called the baptism of the Holy Spirit. Charismatics believe that spiritual maturity and speaking in tongues go hand in hand. They see the gift of tongues as something that can be learned and practiced by anyone seeking it. Some of the ideas within this view include the following:

- Tongues accompanied the coming of the Holy Spirit in several instances recorded in the New Testament, including the Day of Pentecost, the salvation of Cornelius's household, and the baptism of some believers in Ephesus (see Acts 2:1-4; 10:45-46; 19:1-7).
- Tongues are a spiritual language (either ecstatic utterances or an actual unknown language) that is spoken publicly with interpretation for the edification of the church or privately without interpretation for the encouragement of the individual.
- Paul's comments in 1 Corinthians 14 validate that speaking in tongues can be a private religious experience all believers should seek. Paul said that he wished everyone spoke in tongues (14:5) and that the church was not to forbid speaking in tongues (14:39).

3. Continuationism. Those who hold this view believe that all spiritual gifts continue to be in use today but that we should be careful to practice them according to the Scriptures. Some of the ideas within this view include the following:

- Opinions vary concerning whether the gift of tongues includes only authentic languages or ecstatic utterances as well.
- The gift of tongues is not associated with spiritual maturity, Holy Spirit baptism, or salvation. Not everyone has the gift of tongues because the Holy Spirit decides which gift(s) to give each person.
- To maintain order in the church, speaking in tongues publicly requires that biblical guidelines of interpretation are followed and no more than three speakers are permitted.

No matter how you understand the disputable details regarding tongues, we can find unity in discussing these ideas with humility, respect, and the understanding that one day we will have a much clearer view. Until then, we are to show a watching world that although we do not see eye to eye on every topic, we can live love even when we disagree.

DIGGING DEEPER WEEK 5 HIGHLIGHTS

The Sound of Silence

See AbingdonPress.com/FirstCorinthians for the full article.

In 1 Corinthians 14:34-35 we find these words: "Women should be silent during the church meetings. It is not proper for them to speak. They should be submissive, just as the law says. If they have any questions, they should ask their husbands at home, for it is improper for women to speak in church meetings." These statements can be confusing to us as modern women. In other writings Paul clearly has said that men and women are equal in Christ. To the church at Galatia he writes, "There is no longer Jew or Gentile, slave or free, male and female. For you are all one in Christ Jesus" (Galatians 3:28). So why this instruction to be silent when the church gathers?

There are three main views among Christians regarding the interpretation and application of these verses.

1. **The instruction for women to be silent in the church was related to the cultural conditions of the original audience**. This view tends to be the most commonly held view in church practice today. Similar to Paul's instruction for women to cover their heads, this instruction for women to be silent had some cultural "wrapping" attached to a specific issue related to the overarching principle of order in the church. The focus was on maintaining clarity and order rather than keeping women from participating in worship.

2. **Women can speak but should not teach in the church**. Proponents of this view believe Paul was referring to teaching when he spoke of the silence of women. They cite 1 Timothy 2:12 for scriptural support: "I do not let women teach men or have authority over them. Let them listen quietly." Some who take this stance do not allow women to teach at all, while others permit women to teach children or other women but not audiences of mixed genders.

3. **Women should be completely silent in the church**. Those who hold this stance do not see any culture wrapped in this verse but consider it a binding instruction. Though few traditions hold strictly to this view today, I know a family who left a church because women were allowed to pray and make announcements.

To understand the first view, we must explore the cultural context. It is significant that Paul raises this issue in the midst of reprimanding the church at Corinth for their lack of order. What was going on here?

Christianity brought liberation and hope to women of that time who were considered second-class citizens and did not have access to education. Jesus talked to women freely, which was unheard of in Jewish culture, and encouraged them to learn and grow in knowledge. He told Martha that Mary had chosen the better part in sitting at his feet and listening (Luke 10:42). Throughout the New Testament we see women in the early church leading and exercising their spiritual gifts:

- Phoebe was a deacon in the church who was called worthy of honor and helpful to many. (Romans 16:1-2)
- Priscilla was a co-worker in Paul's ministry who once risked her life on his behalf. (Romans 16:3-4)
- Junia was a fellow Jew who suffered in prison with Paul and was highly respected among the apostles (though there is some debate about whether Junia was female or male). (Romans 16:7)
- Euodia and Syntyche were women who worked hard in telling others the good news. (Philippians 4:2-3)

We also read in 1 Corinthians 11:2-16 that women could pray and prophesy with their heads covered. Knowing the freedom that Christianity brought to women makes this passage about women being silent in church puzzling.

Our responsibility in studying the Bible is to recognize tensions and make theologically informed decisions. When we look at the whole of Scripture, we see that gifts are given to all—women and men alike. In reality, few churches today could say that they follow a literal interpretation of Paul's mandate. In many churches women are doing much in the areas of leading, teaching, and missions. And in most churches women welcome guests, make announcements, pray, or share testimonies of what God has done.

Although Paul instructed women to be silent and ask their questions at home, we must be careful to unwrap the cultural implications of the original audience so that we do not get caught up in the letter rather than the spirit of the law. The question we should ask is "What is God's heart in this?" One plausible explanation some scholars have suggested is that women in the early church were liberated to learn but still had a long way to go in their knowledge and understanding. In their immaturity, they may have been interrupting the order of church meetings with questions that were valid yet so elementary that they were disruptive.

While Christians may disagree about the interpretation and application of these verses about women being silent in the church, we can live love even in the midst of opposing views. Each of us must make our own decisions about how to understand the biblical text and find a local body of believers where we can serve in the way we feel called and equipped.

Week 6

REAL LIFE

1 Corinthians 15–16

Leader Prep

Memory Verses

Thank God! He gives us victory over sin and death through our Lord Jesus Christ. So, my dear brothers and sisters, be strong and immovable. Always work enthusiastically for the Lord, for you know that nothing you do for the Lord is ever useless. (1 Corinthians 15:57-58)

Digging Deeper

Read Digging Deeper Week 6, "Afterlife," and note any interesting facts or insights you would like to share with the group. (See pages 62-63 for highlights; read the full article at AbingdonPress.com/FirstCorinthians.)

Materials Needed

- *First Corinthians* DVD and DVD player
- Stick-on nametags and markers (optional)
- Index cards or sticky notes (optional—Scriptures and Prayer Requests)
- Option 1: items needed for your choice of butterfly craft; Option 2: index cards; whiteboard (or chart paper), markers, and eraser (Optional Group Activity)

Session Outline

Note: Refer to the format templates on page 7 for suggested time allotments.

Welcome

Offer a word of welcome to the group. If time allows and you choose to provide food, invite the women to enjoy refreshments and fellowship. (Groups meeting for sixty minutes may want to have a time for food and fellowship before the official start time.) Be sure to watch the clock and move to the All Play icebreaker at the appropriate time.

All Play

Ask each group member to respond briefly to this question: *What is a childhood memory you have of Easter?* (church, clothes, family traditions, activities, baskets, egg coloring, and so on)

Read aloud or paraphrase:

> *As we complete our study today, we will be looking at some of the most detailed biblical accounts of afterlife. At Easter we celebrate that Jesus rose from the dead, and God wants us to remember that we too will rise! Paul wanted the church at Corinth to understand the temporal nature of this life, because thinking about eternity helps us live differently in the here and now. It gives us perspective for the trials of earth and hope for what is to come, reminding us that one day we will be transformed.*

Digging Deeper Insights

Share insights from Digging Deeper Week 6, "Afterlife" (highlights on pages 62-63; full article at AbingonPress.com/FirstCorinthians). You might consider summarizing some of the Scripture verses and what they reveal about the afterlife. Then ask this question: *How does the Bible's promise of life after death give you hope for this life?* If you choose, encourage group members to read the full article online.

Prayer

Before playing the video segment, ask God to prepare the group to receive His Word and to hear His voice.

Video

Play the video for Week 6. Invite participants to complete the Video Viewer Guide for Week 6 in the participant book as they watch (page 204). (Answers are provided on page 64 of this book.)

Group Discussion

Video Discussion Questions

- How does YOLO living (You Only Live Once) make it difficult for us to drill down deep into the resources of the power of God? How can remembering that we have resurrection power living within us help us live victoriously regardless of our circumstances?
- How does taking the "long view" help us in this life? How can it keep us from causing damage by trying to pull all the weeds we see in others' lives? Why is it important to speak truth carefully and sensitively? How can we know if God is calling us to speak truth to someone?
- Why does God sometimes allow us to struggle? What does this accomplish in us?
- How does it encourage you to know that nothing we do for the Lord is ever useless?

Participant Book Discussion Questions

Note: Page references are provided for those questions that relate to specific questions or activities in the participant book.

Before you begin, invite volunteers to look up the following Scriptures and be prepared to read them aloud when called upon. You might want to write each of the Scripture references on a separate index card or sticky note that you can hand out.

Scriptures: John 11:25; 1 Corinthians 15:1-11; Psalm 16:8-11; Isaiah 53:3-10; Matthew 12:38-41; 1 Corinthians 15:12-19; 2 Corinthians 11:24-27; Romans 8:18-25; 1 Corinthians 15:35-42; 1 Corinthians 15:43-57; 1 Corinthians 15:58; 1 Corinthians 16:1-4; 1 Corinthians 16:5-9; James 4:13-15; 1 Corinthians 16:13-14

Day 1: The Main Thing

- Read John 11:25. What did Christ say about Himself? (page 176)
- Read 1 Corinthians 15:1-11. What is one of your earliest memories of believing in Jesus? If it seems you always have believed, share one of your earliest memories of hearing about, or praying to Jesus. (page 177)
- Read Psalm 16:8-11, Isaiah 53:3-10, and Matthew 12:38-41. What do these verses teach us about Christ's death, burial, and resurrection? (Refer to page 178.)
- How has God used His Word in your life recently to confirm truth or direct your thinking? (page 178)

Day 2: YOLO

- Read 1 Corinthians 15:12-19. How did you fill in the blanks on page 181?

- If someone asked you why the Resurrection is vital to the Christian faith, how would you answer? How does hope in Christ for the next life give you encouragement in your daily struggles in this life? (page 181)
- Read 2 Corinthians 11:24-27. Paul had many trials. What are some trials that have caused you to look forward to heaven? (page 182)
- Read Romans 8:18-25. How do these verses from Romans encourage you in the midst of whatever difficulties you are facing? (page 183)

Day 3: Nothing Wasted

- Read 1 Corinthians 15:35-42. What were some of the illustrations Paul used for the Resurrection, and what insights did you gain from them? (Refer to the chart on page 186.)
- What are the realities of your "tulip bulb" life? What is one thing about having a resurrected body that you are looking forward to? (page 187)
- Read 1 Corinthians 15:43-57. What are some things you learn about earthly and heavenly bodies according to these verses? (Refer to the chart on page 188.)
- Read 1 Corinthians 15:58. What have you been doing lately that seems to be a waste of your time, talents, or treasures? (page 190) How does this verse encourage you?

Day 4: Living and Giving Love

- Read 1 Corinthians 16:1-4. What giving principles did you learn from these verses? (Refer to the questions on page 192.)
- Read 1 Corinthians 16:5-9 and James 4:13-15. What opportunities currently are before you? What flexible plans might the Lord be calling you to make? (page 194)
- Refer to page 194. What were the two main principles from today's lesson? Which one did you put a checkmark by, and why?

Day 5: Loving People

- Who is a mentor in your faith journey? Who are the people in your life God has called you to invest in? What is a practical way you can invest in one of these people this week? (pages 196–197)
- How do you respond to other believers when you see a subject differently than they do, especially if it has to do with people you love? Do you have a tendency to compete and compare, or do you choose to collaborate? (page 197)
- Read 1 Corinthians 16:13-14. How do these truths resonate in your life and relationships right now? (page 200)
- Look at the final Weekly Wrap-up together. If some women didn't do the exercise, take the time to read through the review chart together. Then ask: Which week's themes echo into your current circumstances? Why? (pages 201–202)

Optional Group Activity (for a session longer than sixty minutes)

Option 1: For those who are crafty, check online for ideas for making a butterfly craft that ladies can take home with them to remember God's transforming power. (Search for "butterfly crafts" and choose from many wonderful ideas—from simple to more elaborate.) You might consider having each participant chip in a small amount for supplies.

Option 2: Play a game of Pictionary or charades using these or other words from our study. Write the words on index cards in advance. For Pictionary, you also will need a whiteboard (or chart paper), markers, and an eraser.

body, building, ships, water, tent making, temple, eye, ear, hand, foot, butterfly, mirror, gold, silver, jewels, wood, hay, straw, flames, food, yeast, marriage, world, idol, shepherd, soldier, seed, plant, drink, gifts, tongues, instruments, cymbal, love

Prayer Requests

End by inviting the group members to share ways that God has been at work during this study, including answers to prayers that you have prayed for one another. After giving God praise and thanks, invite Him to continue working in each of your lives as you seek to live love—especially when you disagree.

DIGGING DEEPER WEEK 6 HIGHLIGHTS

Afterlife

See AbingdonPress.com/FirstCorinthians for the full article.

Most worldviews propose some ideas about what happens after death. The Greeks believed in the immortality of the soul after the body died. Others claim existence ceases upon death. As followers of Jesus, our hope for the next life is based on what we find in the Word of God.

We look to the whole of Scripture to inform our understanding of afterlife, acknowledging that some mystery still remains. The Bible gives us glimpses of another world but not a complete picture. For now, our view is partial and incomplete (1 Corinthians 13:12). If we think our understanding is puzzling, the Old Testament followers of God had even less revelation. Here are just three verses in the Old Testament that reveal little hope for the next life:

For the dead do not remember you.
Who can praise you from the grave? (Psalm 6:5)

What will you gain if I die,
if I sink into the grave?
Can my dust praise you?
Can it tell of your faithfulness? (Psalm 30:9)

For the dead cannot praise you;
they cannot raise their voices in praise.
Those who go down to the grave
can no longer hope in your faithfulness. (Isaiah 38:18)

As in each of these verses, the word *grave* is used often in the Old Testament to refer to a "holding place" of the dead called *Hades* (Hebrew) or *Sheol* (Greek). While the place of the dead was not a fully developed concept, it does seem that within the dead there was mention of a good place (Abraham's bosom, paradise) as well as a bad place of suffering (hell). Both were temporary places. Some believe that after Jesus' death on the cross, he emptied paradise and brought the people there to heaven. Hell is also a temporary place that ultimately will be thrown into the lake of fire (Revelation 20:14).

Though Hades or Sheol was not a developed theological concept, we do find hope for life after death in the Old Testament. In addition to King David's reference that he would see his dead child again (2 Samuel 12:23), there are other passages such as these:

"But as for me, I know that my Redeemer lives,
  and he will stand upon the earth at last.
And after my body has decayed,
  yet in my body I will see God!
I will see him for myself.
  Yes, I will see him with my own eyes.
  I am overwhelmed at the thought!" (Job 19:25-27)

"But those who die in the LORD *will live;*
  their bodies will rise again! (Isaiah 26:19)

"At that time Michael, the archangel who stands guard over your nation, will arise. Then there will be a time of anguish greater than any since nations first came into existence. But at that time every one of your people whose name is written in the book will be rescued. Many of those whose bodies lie dead and buried will rise up, some to everlasting life and some to shame and everlasting disgrace." (Daniel 12:1-2)

We see that the Old Testament view of afterlife was limited but far from nonexistent. In fact, the above verses line up with New Testament teaching about bodily resurrection. Nowhere in Scripture do we find a more detailed account of a future resurrection than 1 Corinthians 15. Here we find this order: Jesus was raised from the dead as the first of a great harvest (1 Corinthians 15:23); when He returns, all who belong to Him will be raised (1 Corinthians 15:23); after that the end will come and the last enemy to be destroyed will be death (1 Corinthians 15:26). A few other New Testament passages lend more information about afterlife:

"And they will go away into eternal punishment, but the righteous will go into eternal life." (Matthew 25:46)

"But now, as to whether the dead will be raised—even Moses proved this when he wrote about the burning bush. Long after Abraham, Isaac, and Jacob had died, he referred to the Lord as 'the God of Abraham, the God of Isaac, and the God of Jacob.' So he is the God of the living, not the dead, for they are all alive to him." (Luke 20:37-38)

Yes, we are fully confident, and we would rather be away from these earthly bodies, for then we will be at home with the Lord. (2 Corinthians 5:8)

While many disputable details exist about the next life, what we do know from Scripture is that Jesus made us righteous in the sight of God through His blood shed on the cross. We can rest in knowing that those who have called on the name of the Lord will enter the presence of the Lord and their bodies will be raised at His second coming. Paul said in Philippians 1:21, "For to me, living means living for Christ, and dying is even better." One day death will indeed be swallowed up in victory. As we contemplate our own deaths and the deaths of people we love, we must rest our confident hope on God's promises to raise us again to new life and to ultimately conquer death.

VIDEO VIEWER GUIDE ANSWERS

Week 1

    unity matters
    harmony / united
    unity / uniformity
    shared identity
    holy
    heaven
    Holy Spirit
    optimism

Week 2

    warn / children
    spiritual diet
    get along
    eternity
    humility
    power / talk

Week 3

    follow / culture
    bodies
    discern / best
    focus
    distractions
    stumble
    love / strengthens

Week 4

    rights
    agents / love
    common ground
    halfhearted / training

Week 5

    love / be loved
    people
    conflict
    partial / incomplete
    His way

Week 6

    resurrection / victorious
    bad / good
    hope / bigger
    glorious bodies
    useless

Made in United States
Troutdale, OR
10/11/2024

23668253R00038